FRANK LLOYD WRIGHT:

HIS LIVING VOICE

The Press at California State University, Fresno

FRANK LLOYD WRIGHT:

HIS LIVING VOICE

SELECTED AND WITH COMMENTARY

BY BRUCE BROOKS PFEIFFER

Second Printing

Printed in the United States of America

LC #87-62413

Edited by Carla Jean Millar
Production supervisor: Rosie Gutierrez
Audio technician: Ray Freeman

Orders should be addressed to:
The Press at California State University, Fresno
Fresno, CA 93740

Dedicated to the memory of Jeanne Satin,
beloved wife of my friend and publisher Joe Satin,
who made this and other books possible.

ACKNOWLEDGMENTS

For permission to use the photographs in this
volume, my grateful thanks to the following:

Courtesy of Y. Futagawa and Associated
Photographers, photos by Y. Futagawa:
Darwin D. Martin; Unity Temple, skylight detail;
Samuel Freeman house, corner window detail;
S.C. Johnson & Son Administration Building;
Toufic Kalil house; Marin County Civic Center;
Hillside Drafting Room, detail of wood trusses;
Fallingwater; Loren Pope house;
Solomon R. Guggenheim Museum

John Engstead: Frank Lloyd Wright 1954 portrait

The Frank Lloyd Wright Memorial
Foundation: for all remaining photographs used
in this volume

CONTENTS

  *These selections are included on the cassettes.
**cassette only

[Ed. note: My aim in these selections has been to adhere as closely as feasible to a word for word presentation of each talk. In the few cases where omitted words or phrases are vital to understanding, I have added them in brackets to indicate that they are not part of the original text. In the case of words or phrases half begun, then exchanged for more felicitous ones, I have given the speaker's final choice. In the main, however, all texts in this volume echo the actual sound of the living voice of Frank Lloyd Wright.]

B.B.P.

PREFACE

Sunday mornings he would come in at 9:00, resplendent in a suit tailored by Stevens of Chicago, a shirt tailor-made by Budd of New York, his pork-pie hat made to order by Geulot of Paris, swinging the familiar malacca walking stick. We of the Fellowship were all there, dressed in our Sunday best, as was the dining room, with fresh flowers and furniture newly arranged, everything fine tuned to create a special air for this special occasion.

Whatever the table arrangements, Frank Lloyd Wright was always seated at the core, accessible to all. Accompanying him was Mrs. Wright and whichever guest or guests were on hand at the time. As breakfast came to a close and he sensed the anticipation in the room, he would smile in a way that seemed to light up his whole being and say to us: "Quiet seems to be descending upon the house. When quiet descends I suppose it's an invitation for somebody to speak. And I am afraid that somebody is me!" Then he would begin to speak in his deep, compelling, ministerial voice—commonplaces at first: the introduction of a guest, compliments on the flower arrangements, exchange of pleasantries. Soon however the greatest architect of the century would rise to his special level and talk to us about his life, the workings of his mind, his views on America and the world, and architecture, always architecture, the matrix from which all things derived and to which they invariably returned.

The talks were always spontaneous, although once in a while he would read something to us which he had been reading himself. Subjects could derive from guests then present, visitors such as Carl Sandburg, Solomon Guggenheim, Henry Luce, Serge Koussevitsky, Charles Laughton, Margaret Sanger. In Taliesin West, in Arizona, he would often speak of desert things and of the principles at work in nature there. In

Taliesin North, in his beloved Wisconsin, he would remind us of when as a boy he felt the mud of the prairie soil between his toes and dreamed of forms that would one day become great buildings.

The "we" who listened to these talks almost every Sunday were the Taliesin Fellowship, that group of apprentices, young men and women, who came to Taliesin to study architecture under Frank Lloyd Wright. Most of them would study a year or two and then go out on their own to carry forward the principles they had learned. Some of them, myself included, would stay on and hear his Sunday talks across the years in all their endless variety.

I began recording the Sunday talks in 1950—others had done so earlier, producing recordings that date from 1948. My equipment progressed from a simple tape recorder all the way up to stereophonic sound systems with multiple microphones. Through it all, the high level of these Sunday talks remained constant, and for this volume I have tried to set forth as best I can the life and thoughts, the world and universe of a most articulate genius. It has not been easy. For one thing, the possible choices are richer than any one book can hold. For another, to present each of the four Parts of this book in penetrating view I have had to select in tight, inevitable sequence, when memory urges me to add another excerpt here, another couple there. By way of compromise a "Summing Up" section has been added, consisting of two far ranging talks wherein the curtain opens to its fullest extent. One of them, "Really To Believe in Something," is one of the gems of the collection. Equally worthy is "The Master Poet," which occupies all of Side Four of the cassette tapes but is omitted from the text. By thus leaving you, the reader, alone with the living voice of Frank Lloyd Wright we hope to recreate for you, at least in part, the first hand experience of those Sunday talks. As further compromise the cassette tape originally planned to accompany this volume has grown to two. Thus several selections from each Part, plus a complete "summing up" talk, can be heard as we heard them long ago at Taliesin, and on Sunday occasions still do.

How much of what Frank Lloyd Wright told us, so freely given, so openly shared, actually took root in those of us who had the great good fortune to hear him? In a talk given near the end of his life he told us "how the little thing that you didn't notice grows to be the big thing that you talk about and stand by thirty-five, forty, fifty years afterwards." For myself I must say that now, more than thirty-five years later, I find in listening to the talks, or reading the transcripts of them, that ideas and statements which interested me then, now come into clearer focus and with a richness of understanding that only time and experience can yield.

And the "little thing" referred to has truly grown to become the "big thing."

It was a wonderfully rewarding experience to have been present in the same room as Frank Lloyd Wright those Sunday mornings. But now I realize that the things he said have had to run their proper course. They could grow and intensify in meaning only as a person himself grows with the passing of years. And I think I speak for Frank Lloyd Wright when I say that such a flow of ideas, impressions, insights on a myriad of subjects are not merely doled out for the asking, but dearly earned through hard work, suffering, time, and love.

PART ONE

AUTOBIOGRAPHY

For most of us the measure of our lives is what seems to us most real, a grab bag mixture of things done and things witnessed, the whole lightly dusted with shaking outside events. The Frank Lloyd Wright "Autobiography" that follows stands in striking contrast to the ordinary way. Its unit of measure from first to last is architecture, the hub around which his experiences, observations, and the world outside all revolved. His self became his buildings, and everything he did and saw and ever learned was funneled into them.

> I'll live
> As I'll work
> As I am

began a work song that he wrote as a youth and referred to all his life.

Architecture for Frank Lloyd Wright was not only all in all but also God's will. I remember when, for his 80th birthday, we gathered to share breakfast with him in the large studio in Taliesin, a lofty two story room first built in 1911. Over the years it had been changed and enlarged, but basically it was the room in which such designs as Midway Gardens, the Imperial Hotel, Fallingwater, and the Johnson Wax Building had seen the light of day. On this particular chilly morning in June, with a good fire blazing in the fireplace, Mr. Wright spoke of this studio in the context of his life and work. He spoke of the two fires that had demolished the living quarters of Taliesin. Then he pointed to the entrance of the loggia, where the studio was joined to the house. "There, at the loggia doorway," he said, "is where the fire stopped both times, reducing my living quarters to smoke and ruin, but sparing the studio. It was as if God questioned my character, but never my work."

Of the 289 Sunday talks that we have recorded, plus summaries of talks remembered from years before, we glean little of what by ordinary standards would be classed as autographical. Yet indeed every talk he ever gave us was about his life, a life absorbed into buildings that live. Their variety, their beauty, their innovative contributions comprise his very being, a three dimensional legacy for all to see.

Indicative of the man was his belief that architecture could free and inspire humankind, and he infused that belief not only into his houses but also into his great commercial works. The Johnson Wax Building, for example, created so superior a working condition that the company showed a marked increase in level of production and quality of personnel. Herbert Johnson, President of the company, noticed that when the building opened in 1939, "People I wanted to get into the firm and who had refused earlier were now coming to me, wanting to join the company and work in the new building."

Indicative too was his concern for every residential work, regardless of size or cost. For the stately mansion, Wingspread, designed for Herbert Johnson in 1937, 165 working drawings were made. During that same year, for a $5,500 house designed for Herbert Jacobs, Frank Lloyd Wright made 76 drawings. And why not, since each and every house he built was an extension of his very self.

The selections that follow delineate that self. Beginning with a childhood reminiscence, they go on to span almost three-quarters of a century of work. His initial awe at daring to call himself "architect" soon gave way to the breakthroughs he contributed to the profession, beginning with the Winslow house, the Willits house, the Larkin building, Unity Temple. Bold and brilliant innovation would continue all his life, a life measured out by prairie houses, by magic handling of interior space, by a renaissance of later masterpieces, by a series of final visions, some realized others still to be born: the Mile High skyscraper, the Guggenheim Museum, the Baghdad Opera House, the Marin County Civic Center.

Part One concludes with an excerpt from the last Sunday talk he gave us. In it he plans a picnic supper, and after the talk we all journeyed into windswept mountainous terrain with only a vast expanse of desert foliage as far as the eye could see. There we gathered around Mr. Wright in the shelter of lichen-covered boulders, feasting on roast lamb and witnessing the glorious desert sunset. Eighteen days later, on April 9, 1959 the buildings became the man.

Father as Preacher

My father was a preacher in Weymouth, Massachusetts. When I was about seven we were on the way to church. I was walking along with my father and my mother. The home we had to live in was about three blocks from the church. Half way there my father discovered that he didn't have on his necktie, and of course a preacher without a necktie was unthinkable. So he gets the key to the house from mother and runs back. The key won't work—got the wrong key—broke in through a window, got his necktie on and was coming back again with a bleeding finger. That was fixed up, and then we got to church.

I always sat right down low in front of my father, in the front pew of the church. And I looked up at him and I saw him differently somehow from anything I'd ever looked at before, up there in the pulpit with a little something my mother had put around his finger. And do you know he didn't seem at all formidable after that. Didn't seem like a preacher. He seemed quite like one of us, and I never, I think, profited so much by what he had to say after that.

Now is that right, or wrong? It's nature, isn't it. What's that old saying, familiarity breeds contempt. Now you see, without a necktie, with a bleeding finger, having to rush through a window and come back out of it, and then get up there in the sacred atmosphere of the pulpit—well it was just too much for his son! So ever since that time, somehow or other the clerical attire, the neck-cloth and all that has seemed different.

(September 7, 1958)

As Longhair

Your silhouettes are all I see this morning and they remind me of how we are truly the modern Romans. You see the Romans were the first people to put the razor on the scruff of the neck and take the hair off from behind the head where nature never intended you to see it. It's been my proud boast, all my life, that no barber ever put his razor on the scruff of my neck. But there is hardly a town where I've ever been in where I haven't been invited to get my hair cut. They've called across the street, I remember it time and again, "Get your hair cut!" Well, you all have your hair cut and the profiles are quite Roman always, too, if you'll notice now that I've called your attention to it. I think you'll see it for yourselves if you're familiar with Roman coins and the Roman aspect. We are the modern Romans and all that means, I guess.

(December 21, 1958)

As "Architect": the First Time

Architects, I've found, are a hungry species. So hungry. So eager— they're babies back home and they're all kinds of things happening. Probably most of them dodging the sheriff, playing checkers on their coattails, having an awful time of it and here comes a job. Hmmm. Well, what are you going to do about that? I used to have the boys in after they'd been with me for a while and I'd see them backsliding when they got a building to build and I'd say, "Well, now here this isn't what I devoted myself to you for, and you to me, for so many years. What's the matter?" "Well," he said, "Mr. Wright, you know we have to live." And I'd say, "I don't see why." If you have to live at the expense of something to live, why don't you go out and dig ditches? Make an honest living. Because it's dishonest to betray the thing that you feel is the right thing, for money.

And I believe that's what's the matter with the architectural profession today. The older I grow—and I can speak freely because I have refused to join the A.I.A., all my life—didn't want to accept the Gold Medal, but did because I didn't want to be a cad. And they said when I took it they thought I was going to be one of them. And they thought it made me one of them—but they were wrong. And they said, "Now, Frank, you'll be one of us, won't you?" And I said, "Yeah—just the way I've always been!" So I am. They never asked me for anything I didn't give except that—joining them and making a harbor of refuge for the incompetent. Giving a high name to something that didn't deserve it. Now that's the basis of the arrogance that I'm famous for. That sort of thing. Not being willing to sell out. Now you'll be classified as arrogant if you don't want to sell out. I think selling out is the basis of humility as it's understood in our country. So look out.

Being an architect is something that was different. I felt, of course, that I was given a great mission and that there was something even above the priest, the preacher, akin to the prophet—he was a great form-giver for his people, his civilization. And when I put that name "Architect" on a glass door, which by the way was about the first glass door ever done, *[it]* came crashing down the first week after it was put up because somebody slammed it too hard—and the letters came down with it. Gold letters. I sit out there in the hall looking at it, and I thought I had a terrible nerve to put that thing up there, you know. I felt kind of like an imposter. That's the feeling I had about architecture when I went into it. Well, that's what it is, too.

Should be, and isn't. And you see the judges and everybody nowadays regarding it as a business and the Supreme Court of Wisconsin referred to my design business here with you boys—my "design business." Well, you see, that's the fault of the profession. You can't call it the fault of the people. How are they going to know if an architect, a young fellow is supine and hungry and necessitous and will sell out and do anything they want him to do. Well, what is he? What idea are they going to get of what constitutes a proper architect?

So they've got the wrong idea from the architects themselves—they didn't get it from anywhere else. The architects have done this thing to themselves and there's no denying it. And that's why I've never joined them—never wanted to be a party to that degradation of a great idea, a great factor in society. Well, I've done more, I'm sure, about being independent of it than if I'd been of it. I would have been dragged into this same thing. So I wouldn't advise many of you to join the architectural profession as it now stands unless you want to do as Guthrie, my friend of St. Mark's in-the-Bouwerie in New York City, a brilliant man, one of the best minds I've ever known. And I remonstrated with him for staying in the Episcopal Church with his liberal ideas. And "Frank," he said, "I can do more inside of it to change it or destroy it than I could ever do outside." So maybe that's the reason why you fellows *should* join the architectural profession. Get in it and change it or destroy it.

(May 22, 1955)

The Early Houses

Now, I haven't a thought in my head this morning to talk to you about. And if you've any thoughts in your heads, well, come forward with them and I'll talk on the subject. It's quite easy to talk along any line for a little while. What does somebody suggest as a subject?

Apprentice: Mr. Wright, after you worked for Adler and Sullivan for seven years you started out and you did mostly homes—houses?

Yes.

Apprentice: And all the time with Adler and Sullivan the work for the firm was of a different character, apparently. Why didn't you do some of that work you started?

Nobody seemed to ask me. I had an idea that an architect was quite an elevated personage and people came to him, and if they didn't come to him and he went to them, why, he was theirs—he did what they wanted. But if they came to him, why, he could do what he thought they should have. So never in my life have I ever asked anybody for a job. Most architects, while they have that as an idea, never practise it. That's why I never joined the profession when I found that out. I didn't want to join because I thought they were all prostituting the character of an architect. I had grown up from childhood with the idea that there was nothing quite so sacrosanct, so high, so sacred as an architect, a builder. And I suppose that was the foundation perhaps of the subsequent reputation for arrogance which I earned. It wasn't really arrogance, it was only faith and confidence in what I had to say, do and give if they came to me. But I couldn't go to them. That's the story. That's why I've kept on building houses.

I built the Winslow house. It was a terrific sensation; the whole town would stream around that way on Sunday and the place was so crowded with people that they couldn't finish it without putting up bars and keeping people out.

Same thing with the next house I built. And then, Mr. Moore, who was a lawyer and a very sensitive, reputable gentleman, came to me for a house and said he didn't want anything like that Winslow house so he would have to go around back ways to the train to avoid being laughed at. So he got a half timber house. He brought me a cut, a little illustration of the house he wanted, to make sure he didn't get anything like that Winslow house. Well, he didn't get anything like it, but he got a porch on a half timber house, which never happened before. He always thought that house was good half timber. That was the third house I had done.

There is a little story connected with this that I have told and it was printed. I lived diagonally across the street from Mr. Moore, and it became known that he wanted to build a house. I wished, I hoped that he would remember me and come across the street, but there was no sign of it. Several weeks passed, no Mr. Moore, and I gave it up. I had a plate glass door in the office with my name on it. I could see anybody coming. One day there were Mr. and Mrs. Moore standing outside. Well of course I jumped up and fell over myself to get the door open and get them in. I sat them down opposite me at the big table in the center of the room and said, "Mr. Moore." And he said, "Mr. Wright, you know I've been wanting to build a house, and every architect I ever heard of and a good many I never heard of have been to see me to ask me to build that house. And here you live right across the street and I never heard from you. Why?" "Well," I said, "it's simple. You're a lawyer, you're a professional man. I'm a professional man. If you heard somebody was in trouble, would you go to them and offer them your services?" "Ah," he said, "I thought that was it. Well, now we want you to build our house."

That's been the case ever since. There never has been anybody living who even said I asked them to say a good word for me to anybody who wanted to build a building. So I had to pay the penalty. The other boys were rushing around with their qualifications and were good job-getters and I was just a hater of getting a job that way. So I sat around for fifteen, twenty, maybe thirty years waiting, because this country is not so organized that people appreciate that sort of thing. And I merely got the reputation for being high-hat, standoffish, non-cooperative and dangerous. That was the result of it.

There's the answer to why I did not get other buildings to build, and isn't it a little strange that my early experience was all in the theater. I went to Adler and Sullivan during the building of the Chicago Auditorium and did the finished drawings for it. Then came theater after theater. Adler and Sullivan built over thirty when I was with them. I knew acoustics, all that Dankmar Adler knew, and he was the master of acoustics in this country, recognized as such. My early training was all in the theater and nobody's ever asked me to build a theater until just now, in Dallas, Texas. That isn't quite true. Aline Barnsdall asked me to build one and I made the plans for her, but she wasn't the man to build a theater. She didn't build it, it's just a sketch, just a study.

So much for all my early experience, and this applies in answer to your question—though I was perfectly trained for the job, nobody asked me to build a theater. All these years, and I sat around here with a worm's eye view of society for fifteen years, getting a little job here and a little job there, maybe. I didn't go out after a job, I never asked anybody for one I wanted. But if I hadn't lived a long time, it would all have vanished. What I held so high as a professional standard of honor was going to completely snuff me out unless I could live a very long time. So here we are. Now is that the answer?

I don't believe that it is quite as bad now as it was then. And yet I think it is, because the big work today, the important work, government work, like the Air Force Academy for instance, and all these high, important, tall buildings, are done by the plan factories—by the commercial concerns, by those concerns who are equipped to wield statistics and have a line of salesmanship that impresses the businessman because they're founded on figures, not on anything particularly architectural. So it goes now that architecture is drifting toward the big business, and the businessman who has an architect's office with three or four or five hundred draftsmen in it is the man who really is the bellweather of the profession. He wields the power that you see manifested all through the country, in these buildings that are built without any soul, because you can't do much with a soul in the plan factory. It gets in the way.

When I was with Adler and Sullivan they were doing big office buildings and large buildings and they wouldn't take residences. Residences, well, it took as much trouble and fuss to build a good house as it took to build a big office building, more. They threw them out; they couldn't afford to do houses. So when a friend turned up and wanted a house and asked Adler and Sullivan to build one, they turned it over to me. I'd take it home and bring the plans in, and that was that. So I was a house specialist, even when I was with Adler and Sullivan. I did Louis Sullivan's own house for him, down at Ocean Springs. Then I did his brother's house, Albert, down at the South Side. I did the Charnley house, for his friend Charnley. I did McCarg's house and the Winslow house—it was an Adler and Sullivan contract. I also designed one for James Miller. They were all contractors in the Adler and Sullivan office, so those direct contacts were what I had and that's how I happened to get the work. But I do not recommend the process now to you, this waiting process. It's pretty difficult, especially when you have a family and the children have to eat—and they keep getting here, coming from somewhere, God alone knows where.

I suppose there is a reasonable medium, a mean. You've heard about the golden mean, haven't you? The two words don't go very well together because mean and golden aren't too compatible. But where would the golden mean lie in this matter of securing a job? Is it all right to get it by hook or crook? That's the way most of them are gotten. I suppose all these boys who've gone out could shed some light on the subject. I don't know much more about it than I did fifty years ago, except that I know being a controversial item you can never build anything for the government. Because all government has its eye on the next election, and they might displease somebody if they took somebody that was unpleasing to the majority of the people. They wouldn't employ him. I've been there and I know—from experience.

Rex Tugwell was thinking of employing me to go down to Puerto Rico when he was with Roosevelt. They were going to rebuild Puerto Rico. And he said, "Wright, why are you such a controversial item? We would like to employ you, but we don't dare." It was when they'd come in one night to see Broadacre City. I said, "Well, if you don't know why I am a controversial item, I can't tell you." But I was, and that was that, and they never gave me a job. What I could have done with Puerto Rico if they had only have given me a job! Well, that's something to think about now. But they didn't think about it then.

(October 23, 1955)

What's New in Architecture

Frank Lloyd Wright began, early in his career, to destroy the sense of architecture as a constricting box that hems things in. At first, he told us, it was a feeling he had for a more meaningful interior spaciousness. But in his design for Unity Temple in 1906, what had previously been feeling and instinct was now achieved by conscious effort. Walls became screen-features, the overhead roof extended out beyond the screen walls, and the reality of the building became the space within.

Apprentice: Why have you made such an abrupt change in the history of architecture, whereas in the past it's always been one style gradually evolving into another?

The reason is simple. You see, the architecture of the past has usually been the product of a long, long civilization—ways and customs developed during ages, centuries, where a fixed way of solving the building problem had become natural: like the Greek or like the Roman or like the Persian or like the Egyptian. It was out of the ground into the light; it was according to the time and the place and the man. And that was its beauty, and that was its strength. But the time changed. The man died and the place stayed there under those conditions. So architecture died with that man. Now in our day comes again the great change, fundamental change, concerning everything connected with life. Nothing is as it used to be.

In order to get the benefit of culture in days gone by, you had to gang up in cities, the closer, the better. And the more the crowd came together, the more crowding there was. And the more culture was disseminated, the more easy it became to get culture. But that all changed when the printing press came in, when we had the book, and when human thought changed from the type of building which used to be the center of interest and culture and the only means it had of dissemination—that all went out. Well, now for 500 years there was a blank. There was the Renaissance which came in, in an attempt on the part of the Italians primarily to bring back the old Greek orders, to bring back the old civilization of the Greeks. So it was called the Renaissance, the re-birth. But art can never be a restatement. And art as fresh and virile and living as it should have been ceased to exist. It all became more or less an intellectual paraphrase, a repetition of what had been under conditions that no longer were. And so architecture virtually died out as a virile expression of time, place, and man.

Well, now here comes this thought of Victor Hugo concerning it. When I was a boy fourteen years old, he got into my attic with this thought—that the Renaissance was the setting sun all Europe mistook for dawn. And that architecture was dead, dying of the book, and that something would have to be done if buildings were going to be built that could be called architecture. Well, I was fourteen when I first read that. It never left me, and I still remember pretty nearly every word of it. I began to think about it, and I felt that soon the Renaissance and all art of the period in which I lived was a good deal like the pilaster. You know what the pilaster is, it's an imitation support pasted against a wall, isn't it. It has no vitality; it has no dignity; it has nothing except a little decorated showiness. Well, that was architecture.

Now I began to see into it as a youngster, and I wanted to go to somebody that thought ahead and that was really modern, and that's how I got to Sullivan. When I got there he had the thought too. Walt Whitman had it; the poets were all having it. I think all the poets of the world had it. Coleridge said, "Such as the life is, such is the form." It was in the air; it was in the blood of the nation too. But it was not articulated.

Then I came along with the feeling that, after all, columns and entablatures and pilasters, all the paraphernalia of the Renaissance, was rubbish. And soon as that entered my young mind, at the time being a radical and a rebel and coming of a radical rebel family, I began to feel that I wanted to fight it and I did. From Sullivan I got a great deal of aid and a great deal of help, because his mind was a really radical mind, a constructive mind. He didn't have this thing that I have now, and that I felt was essential. He didn't care anything about the nature of materials. His imagination was ebullient and rich and he loved his system of ornament, but he had the mind that could see a thing as a whole. And while they were building on buildings, putting one building on top of another, trying to defeat its tallness, he said, "Hell, what's the use? It's tall. What's the matter with a tall building? Make it beautifully tall." And that's what he did. And that was the mind he had.

That kind of mind was what was needed at the time in all this confusion. Because here we were terribly confused. Here we had new tools, new means of making things. It was death to the old order. The old order couldn't live under present conditions. And then there was the Declaration of Independence, freedom of the individual. There was no architecture that fitted that either. It had never been in the world before. It was completely radical, new, so the conditions under which we live now, the time, had changed. The place had changed. And the man had changed.

Well, now it didn't take a very powerful intellect or any very great vision to see that the buildings that were built for totally different conditions wouldn't suit that condition. I never thought it was a revelation or anything of that kind. It just seems to me utter common sense that you shouldn't try to express those new feelings and conditions and the mind of a new man with an old order. So the old order went by the board. Well, now what was new? What would satisfy this change? I had also come against Hercalitus as I came later against Lao-tze, and Hercalitus declared that the only law man could stand by, or would stand by him, was the law of change. You had to know what change meant, where the change was leading, why the change. Well, that was all instinctive where I was concerned. I hadn't been educated along that line. I went to the University of Wisconsin to become an engineer. You can see all sorts of geometrical solutions that used to hang around there, descriptive, geometry, analytical geometry, mathematics this and mathematics that. Never touched the thing. Never learned anything. You could put it all in my eye then and never wink. And today I couldn't remember a simple problem in algebra and do it for you. So that wasn't it.

But getting onto the track where I thought the thing led, I began to try to see what had happened. And the more I got into it, the more I believed that architecture no longer consisted in this thing we call the walls and roof. That wasn't the place to look for it. That was a question of columns and entablatures and this, that and the other things, and I hated it. Instinctively I got to hate it. And then what? All right where is the reality of this thing anyway, what is the truth about the building? And this building *[Larkin building]* was one of the first to express my feeling about it, in 1902. When I felt that the interior space in here—this in which we live— was what was real in the whole building, you see. And you see in this building that the walls around it are not walls particularly. The windows are not punched in the walls. The windows are built out and put against the walls, and they give you the sense of the interior space coming out through. Unity Temple was the same. I had it pretty well in my mind then, and I was going strong. You couldn't touch me with a ten foot pole. I thought I was a prophet, and in a way I was.

Then one day in 1912 I got a little book from the Japanese ambassador to America. The book was by Kakuzo Okakura *The Book of Tea.* This was 1911 or 12, and I was over there in the little drafting room where I'm sitting now, and I read the book. It was a charming little book and all of you ought to own it. It is called *The Book of Tea*. Well, there I read Lao-tze for the first time, and in just so many words I read that the reality of a building does not consist in the roof and the walls but in the space within to be lived in. Well, there was my thesis. I'd been working on it and working on it. Well, I just was like a sail coming down. I thought, my God, after all, 500 years before Jesus this was known. And I had to work it all out for myself. I felt of course very greatly deflated, and I went out on the roads to pound stones and to fix up things as I usually do when I get mentally tired or worn out. It took me days to come to realize that after all, Lao-tze had the theory and said it, but I had built it.

That's how it began, you see. That's when I knew that I was on the right track. After that of course you couldn't touch, you couldn't shake me. I knew where the origin of the thing was. I knew art could never be a restatement. I knew that it had to come from within. And it gradually dawned on me that that was all in line with the Declaration of Independence, that it was according to our Constitution, that there the new man would find his architecture. And there is where he is finding it. I led the way. Mr. Sullivan was on the road also, and if Mr. Sullivan had lived, he probably would have found out this thing too. But he didn't live to find it out.

Now that's what's new in architecture and that's what's new according to what is new in our life today. That's what's new and it has come to us as the democratic ideology of America, of the United States today. What for a free man but a free architecture. What else? Could a free man build those Greek temples any more? Could he put domes up on columns and call it a day? No. He had to have a new sense of what constituted a great building. Well, now that new sense is what you fellows have the benefit of. That new sense of what constitutes a great building is here, and there it is over there, and here it is here, and more or less working wherever you go. You're in it. And as you make yourselves of it, so far, so good. And if you don't, well, nobody's hurt, not even you. It's there for you to get if you can get it.

(May 13, 1956)

Breakthroughs: Prairie Houses, the Larkin Building

The houses Frank Lloyd Wright built in and around Chicago and its suburbs out on the midwest prairie have since been called his "prairie houses." The name is misleading. It must never denote a "style" but rather the solution he found for homes built on the prairie. In them he abolished the dank basement and the cramped attic. And he placed the main living area above the ground level storage, heating and laundry rooms, so that the view along the horizontal prairie would be enhanced.

Certainly the Willits house was the first great prairie house. Here you will find the first statement in modern architecture from grade to coping. What I am saying is where you will find the windows not holes cut in the building, but features planted against the building.

It began to come clear to me in the Larkin building, of course, this idea that the space in the building, in the structure, should come through and be evident as the reality of that building, not the walls and the roof so much. And when you get into this idea of eliminating the containment which is the box, and freeing architecture—setting the walls free and putting to work the screens and the big overhead, reaching out and amplifying space and dragging things in from the outside—you really have entered a new world of architecture which has never existed in the world before.

That is what we are engaged with now in working in different forms, and making practically a new world too. Because the philosophy back of it, of course, as you know, is midway I guess between East and West. It is the West acting upon inspiration and upon a motive which is Eastern, because Lao-tze had this idea first that I knew anything about. And it came down through Jesus and came down through lesser prophets to this day.

Well now, it was never built. You see, it never happened, actually. It was an inner thing. And then Christianity came along with its sentimental distortion of what Jesus really taught, and we have the idea that spirituality is something that is suspended from the sky by sky hooks, and the further you can get from earth the closer to where spirit comes from, up there.

That was not Lao-tze's idea. It was not the idea of the greatest philosophers, because with them you had to start with nature, at least in Organic Architecture now. We feel we must have the ground firm under our feet, and then we can consort with the stars. And we find that spirituality, the real spirit, is a growth from within, from earth upward, not from heaven downward.

So Organic Architecture, you see, takes this thought from within the nature of the thing. It is a profound nature study. And out of all of that are projected these effects, these structures, these ideas, in tangible earth forms, so that life is lived in them and architecture is an experience. All this is genuinely constructive, genuinely new in the history of culture in the world. Well, that will be more and more realized as it goes along and proves itself.

As beautiful building after beautiful building gets itself constructed and built, they will begin to look into it and try to find out what the secret was that kept it perennially young and always working and never let it die because it couldn't die. You see, the product of a principle never dies. The fellows that practise it do, but the principle doesn't.

So here you have in all these structures from first to last a growing idea. And in this work I think it would be well to see the growth of the idea. Now you can see it quite clearly, because I myself looking back upon it now realize where it began to come in, and how it continued and where it was most effective; and where it languished and then again where it picked up. But it is a pretty steady development from the beginning to the end, which is quite interesting when you know how to follow it.

So I think that Ward Willits' house was a beginning. (Harold McCormick saw it when it was built and wanted me to build his house. Harold McCormick was a rich young man at that time driving a great American roadster over the prairie.) Mr. Willits came in and wanted to build a house. We had a little preliminary talk and then I went upstairs and got interested in a building up in the attic and I forgot about him. I left him sitting there. And I came down casually a little later and there he still was. You can imagine my sensation when I saw him in there. What had I done? He was there for half an hour, or more maybe, and I was blissfully unconscious of him up there in the attic working on something. He told everyone after that, "If anything goes wrong with the house I have myself to thank for it because I had plenty of warning."

That was the beginning of the Willits house. Mrs. Willits was a little difficult, of course, like all the wives in the early days—they are not so difficult now. I must say that all the women we build for now are very considerate and enthusiastic, willing to make sacrifices and shy of making suggestions. But it wasn't so those days. Those were the days when I was plugging swinging windows. It is hard for you boys to realize now that the guillotine window was all that existed when I started to build. I called it the guillotine because it went up and down like the guillotine, and it acted like it if you got your neck under it or your hand or something.

But they wouldn't take swinging windows. And the ladies particularly would not have them, because they didn't think they were practical. Well, as I have frequently told you, if it were a case of being practical, and you were trying to substitute for sliding doors a swinging door, I doubt if you could put it over. Think of it. If all doors had been sliding, and firmly fixed and easily rolling, then somebody came along and tried to see you swinging doors, what would your objections be first off? Put yourself in the place of the householder now, and you are familiar with sliding doors and someone wants to give you a swinging door. What would you say?

Apprentice: Keep bumping into them.

Well, that is one thing. What else? Space? Well, there it would be standing there and you might run into it in the dark and split your head open, for one thing. Another thing is that it is at the mercy of the wind that blows. It would bang, slam, and think of the floor space it would take up, to have to sacrifice. You would say, "No, I'll take the sliding door." You couldn't sell anybody a swinging door.

That is the way it is in architecture. These features to which they are accustomed, they are never questioned. Like those windows with which they were familiar. They would take any sort of inconvenience from them because they were established. If you want to throw them out, take something unfamiliar, it might be ever so much better, but they wouldn't be happy with it. That is a feature of human nature that all you young architects are going to encounter, because it isn't going to change in a hundred years, you know, nor five hundred. I guess that is pretty nearly eternal, that quality in human nature. You'll all encounter it.

It is not a question of actual betterment, and you will find many objections to the plans that you make, just like Mrs. Harold McCormick's. Now why didn't Mrs. McCormick like this fresh charming, vital thing that was presented to her? She was a creature of fashion. That hat [she wore], you see, showed the whole thing—her 250 hats, her whole psyche was that of fashion. The house wasn't fashionable, so why should she accept it? She had the money to buy what she wanted, and she wanted something that had that look about it that was fashionable. It was Platt who built the house, finally. Platt was building fashionable houses for New Yorkers along the semi-colonial line. You know the Platt houses.

So that is another stumbling block always in the direction of the consistent development of a good and new idea: fashion. Fashion is of course a case of sham, whether you believe it or not, just as classic architecture is a case of sham. The Renaissance was a sham. Anything is a case of sham that isn't founded upon a principle which is valid, a principle in construction, a principle in nature or a manifestation of it. Outside of that, that lacking, you have a sham. And that is why the State

Capitol in Washington, if you want to come right down to the basis of truth concerning a thing, is a sham. All Renaissance architecture was a sham.

Now in the old Italian world, if you look at the Ducal Palace [in Venice], there was something not a sham. You look across at Sansovino's opus, that was a sham. The tower rising from the square in the Palazzo is genuine architecture, Renaissance, valid. Almost all of the architecture of the Middle Ages was not a sham. The Gothic was not a sham. Nearly everything Renaissance was a sham. And when you get a copy of the copy of the sham, that's a damn sham.

And yet, I must say, I have been a great reader [of Renaissance literature] in my day, used to carry Temple's Shakespeare in my pocket on the train. I've read all of it, all of Shakespeare—had my own idea of the Sonnets. Also read all of George Meredith when George Meredith was considered to be hard reading. And I read Goethe when I was a youngster; read Carlyle's Sartor Resartus when I was fourteen, and by golly, I understood it too, and so forth. So out of books does come a certain question mark. The answers are not in the books. But you can read and read the best of literature, and particularly the poets, and be stirred and inspired in the direction of activity. They will incite you to action, and that is their value. If they don't, they are no good.

Lieber Meister used to say to me, "Wright, read the books, but throw them away." And he was the greatest iconoclast I have ever met, and I met him at the time when he was the freshest. He was just when I needed. He himself, when I first met him was deep in Herbert Spencer, and Wagner was his God in music. He used to sit down and try to play the Leitmotifs of Wagner. He'd hum them when he was working. And later he got on to Walt Whitman.

Well now, what do you want to talk about. This is introductory.

Apprentice: Mr. Wright, when you were doing the Willits house, the picture is right over there beside you, were you conscious then already of wanting to break the box down?

Oh yes, but it wasn't on the surface. It was an instinct. It was something I felt, rather than knew. I didn't begin to know about it until I got to the Larkin building, I think. But I felt it all the time, and I didn't want to do any of those boxes. I didn't know why.

Sullivan never had this feeling I am telling you about the box. You won't find it in all the Sullivan literature. But it was my instinct to feel that about it.

When the Larkin building model first came, that stair tower at the corner was part of the mass, part of the building. And I didn't know what was the matter. I was trying for something with some freedom that I hadn't got. The model was standing on the Studio table in the center, and I came in and suddenly saw what was the matter. I took those four corners and I pulled them out away from the building, made them individual features, planted them. And there the thing began to appear that I was trying to do. You see, I got features instead of walls. I followed that up with Unity Temple where there were no walls of any kind, only features; and the features were screens grouped about interior space. And the thing that came to me by instinct in the Larkin building began to come consciously in the Unity Temple. When I finished Unity Temple, I had it. I was conscious of the idea. I knew I had the beginning of a great thing, a great truth in architecture. And now architecture could be free.

(August 13, 1952)

Larkin Building Innovations

The first steel furniture in the world was made by the Van Doren company of Cleveland for the Larkin building. I was a real Leonardo da Vinci when I built that building, everything in it was my invention. I put the seats on brackets that swung from the desks. Janitors came and cleaned up at night, and there were no waste baskets, no chairs to move, nothing. The Larkin building had in it also the first use of magnesite. We made magnesite bowls and cast all of the ornamental string-courses, sills, and everything in the building. And it was the first air conditioned building in America. We built the ducts into the parapets, and it was thoroughly air conditioned because it was down on the tracks where engines were puffing just outside, continually. It was literally in the railroad yard. So we had to air condition it, and we did. And the first plate glass windows were used there also. Windows of plate glass! It would have been a great thing to have preserved that building, because in it was nearly everything of a modern nature now characterizing modern building.

Magnesite was the old Roman cement. You know why those old aqueducts and old buildings of the Romans have lasted so long was because of the Roman cement, which is really magnesite. It is really a by-product of the soda water fountain. Carbonic acid, gas taken out of it, and you have this thing. The only difficulty is—and we encountered it, and we had to work hard to overcome the difficulty—was that when it sets, it swells, it heats and expands. I think it is the only material of which that would be true. But we made the foot mold so that it could go with it, and when the thing was all cooled off and came down, the mold was still where it should be. I had a Dane named Lauritson on the job who was extremely clever, and who managed that all very successfully.

And there was also, among other items, a suspended toilet partition system. Having got the idea of the water closet up off the floor, I didn't see why all these other things had to be mopped around, and you always see a dirty streak on the floor around them. So I hung it all from the ceiling. It was very pretty and very nice. Quite a nice system. Then I went a little too far with the magnesite thing, and made washbowls out of it, trying to get the plumbing of the building out of the same material the building was built of. Well, that was too far. We found that the soap and the alkali and everything that was used in the bowl deteriorated the bowl. We had to take out the wash bowls and put in stock stuff. So forth and so on. Well, it was great fun.

(January 23, 1955)

Japanese Influences and Froebelian Training

I have never confided to you the extent to which the Japanese print per se as such has inspired me. I never got over my first experience with it and I shall never probably recover. I hope I shan't. It was the great gospel of simplification that came over, the elimination of all that was insignificant. And I had already been made ready for it by Froebel's idea of the kindergarten, you know. This idea that a boy, a child, should not be allowed to draw from nature, to imitate the look of objects until he had mastered the fundamental forms in nature. And that mastery of course was to be had by way of these simple forms, the square, significance of the square which with the third dimension became the cube; the significance of the triangle, which became the tetrahedron; the significance of the circle—give it the third dimension and it became the sphere. And when you had mastered the interplay of those things upon one another, when you had taken them by different angles and revolved them to get subordinate shapes, there you got a a perfect language of form.

Well, now that's the great thing that happened to me when I was a child, a child of seven. Now along with that basic training and, as a matter of fact, I never drew from nature in my life, never wanted to. After I got this and a T-Square and a triangle I had the means of making almost

anything I wanted. And the shading and the shadow and the effects that are incidental all seemed to me beside the mark.

Well, now came manifestation of that very gospel. In the Japanese print shading had been eliminated; there was no, what the Italians call chiaroscuro in anything they did. It was only the form, clear form, and in the print you saw the elimination of everything that was insignificant. As a substitute they had devised what they called *noton,* a gradation of sky, and at the top of the print would always be that *noton,* which was the gradation of the sky coming down. Dark blue at the top shading down into the print, and while it was a mere convention, it gave you everything that sky could ever give you, and you had sunrise, you had mid-day, you had evening, you had night. It was just as simple as that.

Now that was a tremendous confirmation of the Froebelian kindergarten training I had received. So it struck home. And I began to see it taking effect, even in the recording of a national life by a great artist, you see. So in these prints you will see the manifestation of this law of Froebel which declared in its way, in its time, war against the overdoing of the shade and the shadow in the thing that didn't really matter. In other words, realism, I guess you'd call it, wouldn't you? They were anti-realism, the Japanese print. Just as Froebel was anti-realism in training the young mind to see. So here you have a new way of looking at the landscape. And the landscape has never seemed the same to me since I became familiar with the print. You're continually seeing differently; you're seeing, eliminating. You're seeing, arranging. You're seeing, I don't know exactly how to put it. Not in three dimensions, certainly, and yet perhaps that is the element of the third dimension made manifest by two. But you can judge for yourselves. My conscience will be clear as soon as I've revealed to you the source of this inspiration which came to me at a very important time.

Now you may wonder what Japanese prints have to do with architecture? But all that I've been talking about just now refers absolutely fundamentally to architecture as a great art. Because architecture is the basic art from which you can expect painting, sculpture, music to come forth, or go into. It's the natural home of all the great arts, is architecture.

(June 20, 1954)

The Usonian Houses

No commission or task seemed as important to Frank Lloyd Wright as designing homes of moderate cost. Based on the textile-block system of concrete blocks that he had used in California in 1921, he went to work in 1950 to devise a building system that would serve this aim. He called this new method the "Usonian Automatic."

Boys, here is another letter showing where modern architecture is today. I think you have heard me say that modern architecture is in the high school now, haven't you. Such letters as this we get nearly every week, and they come in from the high schools. And most of them are—this is not a typical one, I guess. My goodness, no glasses. Mother, let me use yours. This is from the Shawnee Grade School, Shawnee, Kansas: "Mr. Frank Lloyd Wright, Paradise Valley, Phoenix, Arizona. Dear Mr. Wright: I am an eighth grade boy at Shawnee, Kansas Grade School. My American History class is making a hall of fame of present day patriots. I have chosen you as my 'present day patriot.' Would you tell me who was your favorite American patriot when you were a teenage boy?" Well, who do you think it was? I might as well answer now who my favorite patriot was when I was a teenage boy—Thomas Jefferson. "And what book you liked to read?" That's a hard one. How many of you have got favorite books that you have read? Well, I think I'd have to say Goethe's *Wilhelm Meister*, but I was fourteen then, when I read it first. "Did you have any hobbies at that time and also did you like sports? I know you are a very busy man, but if you can answer my letter I will be very proud to make a report on it. Your friend, Mike Elder."

We get one, maybe two of these, nearly every week from all over the United States saying, "Dear Mr. Wright, we have chosen you for our thesis. Would you send us some helpful material." And here in Miss Elizabeth Gordon's *[editor of* House Beautiful*]* portfolio we have letters concerning the Usonian house from all over the country, too. Plenty of these people have read the book, the new book, *The Natural House,* and they write in. Right away, don't lose any time. And I am sure that we have the nexus there of a great need in our country. As I was telling Miss Gordon, I think it's the lower middle third. We build for the upper middle third. We don't build for the top, for the crust. We build for the upper higher intelligent level of American thought and feeling. They come to us.

Now here comes another strata, anxious, but without much money, probably. They have saved up a few thousand dollars, and they can build a house costing from $12,500 to $25,000. Now beyond that, what they need would actually cost them, if we were to try to do it for them, not less than $30,000, and maybe $50,000 or $60,000. So here in the Usonian Automatic we do have a means by which to do this and for a tremendous number of people. God knows how many millions are in this situation throughout the nation. If we can supply something that will go to that spot, I'll feel that we will have justified our existence absolutely. And of course the process of natural selection is taking place there, because only those people who appreciate a thoroughbred, who know style when they see it, and desire that quality in their lives, would ever take the pains to possess themselves of this means to build a house. Now once they were in possession of it, if there was only some way of getting an agreement for the use of the system according to the designs which should be furnished with it, we'd have an American architecture that would really command the attention of the world, properly. We would have something to be proud of, because one of these when built helps the other.

Every modern, scientific accomplishment, everything that we have achieved in science, in the building industry, is concentrated in this little scheme for building a house. Some of the boys have suggested a block four by eight—that is to say, a sheet—which misses the entire point and throws the whole system away. Because the idea is to get the thing done to a man-handled unit, which any man, any G.I. or some laborers he can pick up, can lift and put up on the wall. So the block we have now, one foot by two feet, is about what could be easily managed. We used to have it sixteen inches square, and I can imagine a block perhaps two feet square could be handled by particularly strong builders. When you get two men on the block, the whole thing is gone, because then comes the suggestions, and the setting of the thing becomes a confusion of labor instead of a concentration of labor. So we are trying out one size unit against another size unit. So far as we've got now it is a man-handled, man-sized block that is the secret of the success of the system.

Now of course steel can run in rods by the mile, the size of your little finger. And to make a larger block would also mean to put less steel in the walls, and they wouldn't have enough steel, really, to give them strength. So the two foot center vertical rod seems to be about what's necessary to give integrity to the building and strength to its surface. You can carry it up fourteen feet high without very much trouble as we've already done, frequently.

Of course the whole thing is a system of design and is an appropriate example of means to an end—and the end is what? A thoroughbred, beautiful piece of architecture that will be there for several hundred years.

The experiments we've made already in Los Angeles *[with four block houses]* indicate no deterioration in this thing whatever. And they were built in 1921, 22. They are already over thirty years old, and not the slightest indication of deterioration can you find in any of them. So, here is a thing requiring no finish, no decoration of any kind except what is in the block. It can be extremely delicate and decorative without anything being put on it. It's all got out of it, and is a part of it, and is indestructible. And there is no maintenance whatever in this type of construction.

The inside, of course, is plywood. Those earlier houses had double walls. The double wall is a great advantage, but it is expensive, unnecessarily so. I think the single wall, with a plywood lining, something like a silk-lined overcoat, would be the thing, and that is what we are going to try now. Now, of course, that plywood lining has all sorts of colors and finishes and anything you want to give it, and your ceiling and walls are the same. Plywood ceiling, plywood walls. And by it setting in a little stud in the block, every second block vertically, and every second block horizontally, it's set to bore those little holes in the ply and put the ply against the block and tighten up with these little circular headed screws. It will look very pretty on the inside of the blocks—something like that car out there with the rivets on the side of it showing. It will make a nice finish, and sufficiently snug and warm for almost any part of our country.

Apprentice: Is there insulation between the block and the plywood?

No. The insulation between the block and plywood won't be necessary, beside the mark. But it can be done, easily. If you want to put paper over there, you can do it. But I think the insulation scheme can be overdone. I think we should have it on the roof. That's the place for insulation, not the walls. And in this case we have an insulated roof that will have about three inches of insulation on top of the block slab, in the roof system. So you have got a pretty snug house. Good enough for any section of the country. If you went very far north, then you might talk insulation; and if you went very far south, perhaps, but I don't know.

We've built in the means of air conditioning boxes, systems now a part of this house and related to the chimney. And the chimney and the air conditioning and all that can be made a part of this naturally and look very interesting, substitutes for the big chimney that I am getting tired of now. I have lived with it long enough. I have been living with that big chimney ever since sixty-five years ago. I have seen it all over the country, and now it's all over the plains here.

They rename things and come out with different names, but they're just the same thing. So in this block system you have the traditional module at work perfectly. You have steel doing its work in tension where it's most economical. You get the most possible out of the steel, and you get the most possible out of the concrete, because you have just enough of it to stand up to fourteen feet. Usually the house will not be higher than nine feet, maybe ten. But you can go to fourteen feet with these small pencil rods with safety. And the roof system requires a little additional reinforcement which can be managed in different ways. The uttermost scientific potential, you might say, of building construction so far is all employed here on behalf of a man who wants to live in a one-room house, wants to live in a modest house.

And the thing has style. That's the point. That is a point which should be considered, and will be, I imagine, by the people who are interested in the superior thing in the way of a building. Usually people who want a superior house want style. And I guess most of them know it when they see it. When you get down below that lower-middle-third strata I don't believe there is very much appreciation for style or desire for it. They are not ready even for this thing that we are talking about. But I think the people who are ready for it are perhaps the most deserving of all of our citizens—the ones who have the least and can get the least because they are the class referred to as those with a "champagne appetite and a beer income." Well, I think this will be for the champagne appetite and the beer income level. That is what we hope.

(January 23, 1955)

The Corner Window and the Johnson Building

By means of the cantilever, bringing the supports in from the corners of the box, the corner was then free to be open. In that open space Frank Lloyd Wright placed windows—the famous corner window—to emit light and air where before there had always been darkness.

There's no real appreciation of what constitutes architecture, of a great building. It is merely fashion now, a new style. But that's what I see. Now I don't know how to fend it off, but I am going to do what I can, to save the day from another style. But that's the habituation of the human mind, prostituted by habit beyond thinking, no longer able to perceive, to envision, to realize—just contented with effects. Now you can take any one of these effects going around the world today. Let's take, for instance, the corner window. It's a conspicuously simple instance.

I perpetrated the first corner window, probably forty-five years ago. What does the corner window represent? I wonder if any of you boys know? You may have heard me tell you this before, I don't know. Have I elucidated the corner window? Well, there was clearly a concept of a view that could establish, well not establish, but could inspire and beget a new world of building.

The Johnson building was the first time I had the nerve to knock it out above. Because if it worked here, why wouldn't it work up there? And it worked. Anyway, now if you go into the Johnson building you're not aware of any boxing in. It is not there. Right where you have always experienced this constriction, you look at the sky. And all that was along the purpose of freeing the interior space, the reality of the buildings that we lived in.

What happened to that basic, generic thought and idea? You could even go now and see them put two corners, one with a window here, like this, with the mullion, and one window here, like this, they moved into the corner, and nothing happened. You can see all sorts of little petty effects and not one realization of the great transformation which took place when that act was performed.

Well, that's only one little incident. We could go through and name dozens, like the overhanging roofs, like the perforated overhang. It's up to you. Someday I hope to see a work with the illustration of these various effects put into their actual significant form. It has never been done. I haven't often talked about it myself—sounds too much like teaching.

(May 28, 1950)

The Grant and Walter Houses

We have just come back from a trip to two buildings that have been going on all winter. We were worried—I was—about the Grant house, because he was with his wife in a stone quarry getting out the stones to build his house with—didn't have too much money but was building about a $50,000 house. And he sent photographs of it and neglected to send or put a human being in the picture to get the scale. So I took the scale to be about like this wall here. And I was alarmed. Then when I saw it the stones were about the thickness of your hand, about as long as two hands, or one hand, sometimes as thick as two hands. And he had produced a remarkably beautiful texture—with stone, no mortar. It was his idea. He put up the forms on either side, of wood. Then he had a little iron bracing in case the sides came up like this, over you, so you could work under them. And he would raise them as the wall went up. And he had a form to give the air space we demanded in the center of the wall that went up with it. And you could take that out. When he came to the sill height or anything, he would fill up the hollow space and plaster it over solid. And it needed no coping, it needed nothing when you got to the top. It was just solid, as though cut out in one piece.

So he has really invented something. And he got the stone out himself, from the quarry. He didn't ask for any help, he and his wife. She shook her head with all of her little short curls. He said she'd cut her hair off so it wouldn't get in her eyes when she was working in the stone quarry. This is an American proceeding, building their own house. And they certainly ought to have a house. They're all tumbled up in a pile with three children, and the parents. But they're getting a lot of fun out of that house. I know. It is going to be beautiful. A new thing in the way of masonry has come to town, because there is no trowel on the face of that thing at all; there is no mortar even. You can stick your hand in about that far all along the outside crevices in that wall. And the color is beautiful of that stone. In the quarry it flakes, a kind of limestone deposit that comes out in little flakes like crackers. So he's going to have a beautiful house. The chimney's finished, and the second story is poured, and he's now busy bending the conduit and putting it in the walls and floor himself. He's no electrician, never had done anything of that kind before. He's a radio man, a very bright fellow. If every G.I. had the wit and intelligence to go ahead and build a house the way he's building his, our colleges would be greatly relieved. Yes, pleasing, astonishing to see what he does.

Then old Lowell Walter, the staunchest guy we've got, he's been two years building his house—this is the third year. He's way off there in Iowa on the river—beautiful site, both of these sites are beautiful, thrilling, magnificent. He is building the *Ladies Home Journal* house. And he's got walnut wood in it, most beautiful walnut I ever saw, with curved edges on it—very expensive. The house impresses you with having been built regardless of money. I guess it was. The house itself, with the boat house— a lovely little building equipped for boats. It has a sliding floor; he pulls them up by a crank out of the river. High water comes, he's prepared for that. He's prepared for everything.

He's a rough old farmer type—he has thirteen farms and he works on shares. He's seldom without that cigar sticking out from his lower lip. Every little detail that man knows about that house. The man has had no education; he's a typical American farm product. Then he got off the

THE GRANT AND WALTER HOUSES   39

farm and he went into contracting. He became a road contractor, building roads. He's a heavy business man with absolutely no education of any kind, and one of the most appreciative clients we ever had. And understanding—he knows, and is he proud of it. My goodness, yes he is.

And when they come down to furnishing it, nothing is too good for it. They're a little worried whether this expensive stainless steel produced by the Swedes was good enough. They suggested silver, and I suggested gold plate! But they'll get along with the stainless steel produced by the Swedes, especially made. And so it goes. The upholstery is all foam rubber that thick. Sit on one of those stools and you go right up to your hip bone. We picked out colors for them, and that's one thing about them; they would not pick out anything unless it was approved. And that's why they've got such a wonderful circumstance.

Now that old fellow, a product of our civilization, has a clearer, finer sense of being than these old so-called aristocrats. And he's gone into the future, way over their heads. There they are, old stick in the muds, back there with something dead, something so dead it smells bad. Now that's the beauty of this country, isn't it? That's what you can do here, and you could never do that in any other nation in the world, I don't think. I don't think even in Sweden. Could you find a farmer in Sweden who without any education whatsoever would put himself into an environment more truly beautiful and exquisite in every detail than the rich people, the titled people? Even the prince himself? You couldn't do it. No, no other country could do that. But I've never seen it so markedly standing out as in this instance of Lowell Walters.

Now undoubtedly the *Ladies Homes Journal* will want to publish that house because they published the original drawings. Here it is accomplished way off in the sticks, in the countryside on a river where almost nobody goes. Quasqueton was once a town; it's now a ghost town practically. And people are already piling in there, coming in. He's embarrassed now, going to learn how to park now that they've discovered the house. And he's getting a great kick out of that too. He likes to be discovered, he likes to be sought out. He feels he's contributing something.

(June 4, 1950)

On Building Permits: the Millard House

What would happen if the country woke up to the fact of what the Usonian type house can do for them. It would be amazing. All kinds, from all stratas of society, not just from young people and G.I.s and that, but from old people who have dreamed of having a house all their lives designed by myself, we'll say. Now, they can have it. Most of these letters that come in say they have $15,000 in the kitty and can't get any more, and some of them say that they're earning from $5,000 to $7,500 a year and they have saved up a few thousand dollars and now they want to build a home. Now they see the chance of their lifetime to build it. So this is really hitting the situation in America, called the housing situation, right square in the eye. It is really a bulls eye, is going to be when it comes out.

Of course, we've been trying to do that all these years. I have. I have been working at this thing since 1921. First house like it was built in 1921. There was a client of mine in Chicago, Alice Millard. Her husband was McClure's old book man, and I built a house for them in Highland Park using board. One of the early board houses. Built it on a unit system—10 inch boards and battens—and then when I came back from Japan in 1920, here was Alice out west wanting a house. So we walked along in Pasadena one day and we saw a charming little ravine, with water in the bottom of it. On each side were two lots for sale, and the ravine didn't seem to have any particular use. So instead of buying an expensive lot on each side, we bought the ravine, which they were glad to get rid of. They didn't imagine anybody was going to build on it, but we did. We built in the ravine. We had a little disaster once, but that's all; it came out all right. And that's the Millard house—the first concrete block house.

I was building it and I didn't have a permit, and they came along after we'd got it about half way up and stopped us. So I had to go and see the building inspector and I got him in the car and drove him out to the place and I showed him what we were doing. "Well," he said, "Frank Wright, this is the best thing that ever came to Los Angeles. This is really fine: it's earthquake proof, it's vermin proof, fire proof, cheap, taken the concrete block out of the gutter and made it something not only interesting but beautiful." And I thought, "Well, this is fine now. I guess I've arrived. We're going to get a permit, we're going to build the house." Then I said, "All right then, Barkis, do we get my permit then to build the house?" "Oh well now," he said, "that's something else. We can't give you a permit—I can't give you a permit. There's nothing to cover this. And if you were to go to the council for it, you wouldn't get it."

And I said, "Why not? You said it was the best thing that has come into the region, why can't I build it?" "Well," he said, "don't you see, here we have what we call in Los Angeles the balance of trade. There are the brick people—they're selling bricks to build with. There are the lumber people—they're selling lumber. What you've done is to give concrete the right of way over all those other fellows. Why, they wouldn't be in the market. You couldn't sell anything after a while if I gave you a permit to go with this thing. You see what the situation is in the building industry." And it is that way. So I was in the dumps again, and I said, "Well, my God, if that's the situation here, what am I going to do?" He chewed on a piece of grass and looked around, and he said, "Why, go ahead and build 'em!"

So, I built them. I built five of them without interference from the headquarters from City Hall, all illegal. Well, it was somewhat worse than laying an egg. That's the origin of the Usonian Automatic house. That's how it was born. I built the Storer house after that up on the hill—a little palace. It looked like a little Venetian palazzo, that house. Then I built the Freeman house. Then there was, finally, the Ennis house, which was way out of concrete block size. I think that was carrying it too far. That's what you do, you know, after you get going, you get going so far that you get out of bounds. And I think the Ennis house was out of bounds for a concrete block house. But the minimum is really the maximum.

(December 12, 1954)

At Florida Southern College

Florida Southern College was an ongoing commission, from 1938 when President Ludd Spivey first contacted Frank Lloyd Wright, until the architect's death in 1959. In his talk he speaks of a visit he made to the College in 1948, when several of his buildings were already built or in construction.

Well, coming home and looking at our boys and girls, we certainly see a contrast to the group at Florida Southern College. They certainly look ragtag and bob-tailed to me, after seeing you. And they behave that way too. I never go down there that the Doctor *[President Ludd Spivey]* doesn't impress me into service and stick me on a platform and talk, when he can. He started me that way, and when he came to Taliesin ten years ago to employ me as an architect, he said he wanted my philosophy as much as he did my ability. So now he makes me shell out whenever I come around.

We had a meeting the evening before the Chapel was filmed, and most of them couldn't get in; it only seats a thousand. So they asked me if I'd speak the next morning. And I had some curiosity about the Chapel's acoustic properties. The piano they had was up on a platform under a low ceiling; it didn't do very well. So I said, "If you'll put the piano down on the floor and have his son play it as a prelude, I'll talk."

That went through and the boy sat down to play the piano, made a very bad selection, I thought. Outside of Bach and Beethoven nothing seems suited to architecture in my mind. He was playing Listz's *Traumerei*; he played it very well. And the students came in, they came in rather late. They began to pile up in the balcony, clattering, making noise, chattering away, till finally you couldn't hear the music. They had no respect whatever, either for the place, or for me, or for the music, or anything else. Just gassing away, girls and boys, and boys and boys. They had thrown their cigarettes away before they got in, and finally the Doctor, who was sitting beside me, shook all over with rage, jumped up and shook his fist at them. And he said, "You be quiet, you be quiet up there, you!" And they all looked kind of startled at the Doc, and kept quiet. He certainly calmed that multitude.

Then we listened to the music which grew more and more sentimental, more and more lingering, with more and more emphasis on sentiment till the end. Then I spoke to them, and I was angry by that time too. Olgivanna said if you want to get a good talk out of me you've got to make me angry. Well, I was angry, and I asked them what they were there for, and how many of them really wanted an education and were there to get one. I said that one-third of them really were there for a serious purpose. And I went on to beat them up. I'm always in the habit of picking on the audience a little, but this was not picking. So there was a great enthusiasm when I got through with the talk.

(August 4, 1948)

A Cure for Gall Bladder Trouble

G.I. Gurdjieff was the radical philosopher and savant under whom Olgivanna Lloyd Wright studied for several years prior to her coming to the United States and meeting Frank Lloyd Wright. In the early years of their marriage Gurdjieff visited Taliesin in Wisconsin, met Mr. Wright for the first time, and a strong friendship developed between the two.

Gurdjieff wanted East to meet West, just as boy meets girl, and he wanted that union of thought and feeling between the Orient and the Western world that could save the world and give us peace. We have never approached that because of our stupidity. We look down upon anything with yellow skin, which is tragic.

Mrs. Beard: And then send it pornography.

He is very wholesome, Gurdjieff, I think. And he was a scientist, he was a physician. He cured me of gall bladder trouble. I was about to have an operation, and he came to me one of the times he was at Taliesin and I had suffered the tortures of the damned, and I was willing to go through with the thing. He came to me at the time, and Olgivanna told him about my pickle, and he pulled down my eye like this, and he looked at it, said "gall bladder?" And he asked us to come to his place in Chicago, and we went. There was dinner. He was a great cook—a millionaire once offered him $25,000 a year just to come and cook for him—he understood things to eat. Well, at that dinner, there was everything hot. Hot food. He would mix salads, mix this and mix that. And he said, "You will have to eat it." Then there was a tall glass, and he filled it with armagnac. In fact, he picked out deliberately everything I had been forbidden to eat! "Eat," he said. "Drink!" Well, I knew I had to have an operation anyway, so I ate. I ate all that hot stuff, and I drank the glass full of armagnac, and I never had drunk any armagnac. And time came to go to bed at night, and I was burning up. My God! Mouth, lips, everything! I said to Olgivanna, "Well, I guess this settles it! You're a widow now!"

And I went to bed, and it took me a long time to get to sleep, but I got to sleep. And I woke up in the morning and good heavens, I felt fine! Burned it out. It was his idea, you see. What he burned out was the idea that I had that I had it. He burned out the idea that I had any trouble with my gall bladder. And for fifteen years I didn't have any more trouble. Then the cat came back, and I did have trouble in the same way fifteen years later. But no gall stones. It was something else. And it was not at all what they had said it was. And if I had lost my little pilot light I wouldn't have been half so well off as I am now. Now, that's Gurdjieff. That is the way he treated everybody. Take them up by the scruff of the neck and fling them in. If they couldn't swim, he would listen to their shrieks with delight.

(March 9, 1952)

Building Codes and the Guggenheim Museum

As you all know, I have just come from the great "cash and carry" into this atmosphere so very different, and I think I should tell you a little something this morning about what is called a code. You all know what a code is? What is a code? Do you know? Well, a code is a series of rules and regulations made to be fool-proof but succeeds only in being rules and regulations for fools. That's really what it amounts to. But Alfred North Whitehead . . . how many of you know of him? He was a professor of Philosophy at Harvard. He was one of the few good men that Harvard has had. He admitted that a democracy had to have a code. But, he said, if it were not fearlessly revised continually, that it would be a menace to democracy rather than a help.

So codes are rules and regulations made by little men to govern middle men. And that's essential, because in a city, of course, the city is divided into blocks. Now, very seldom, if ever, does one citizen get a block. And very seldom, if ever, does one citizen get half a block. He gets a little piece of the block. And if you were to take a loaf of bread and slice it into sections so that every man might enjoy his loaf of bread, you would have to impose regulations on the other fellow who got his loaf of bread, in order that each might have his in peace. So it is with the owner of this little piece of property out of a block. If he's going to enjoy his piece of property in the block, you have got to impose certain regulations like, for instance, the backyard regulation. So they impose upon that man who buys a little piece of property a certain area for a backyard, so that not only can he have light but also so the neighbor man can have light. That requirement adds up in the whole block to quite an area of the block. So it becomes essential to specify and to rule by law, that no man shall have more than a certain use of piece of property—his piece of the pie.

That's all right. But now comes a fellow who buys half a block—no provision was made for him. This is our situation at the Museum, so the backyard regulation does not apply. And yet the amount of ground that you can occupy if you buy a piece of city property is still regulated by the code. So we are in a position in the Museum where we're the equivalent of about five backyards. So we can use only that portion of our second floor which has been allotted by these wise guys who made this provision (as they thought wisely) to restrain the neighbors from. We have to deduct about 4,500 square feet for backyards. Of course the backyard has no application and no relation to the situation. So that's the code.

Now all codes are more or less like that, because it is quite impossible for these imaginations to frame a law, which a code becomes, which doesn't get to be more and more a cast-iron. As you can imagine, every man is anxious to get all he can out of his own piece of property regardless of the neighbor. And the codes have to be relentlessly enforced. That enforcement in the course of years amounts to law. So to try to alter the code is like trying to alter the Constitution of the United States. You can readily see also how injustice should be just about as prevalent as justice in the execution of the code.

That is why Alfred North Whitehead said what he said about fearless, constant revision of the code. Of course, that's troublesome. That requires some higher up not authoritarian—or maybe it does require some authoritarian rulings. Perhaps it is really only a king who can revise a code. But they are constantly being revised—not constantly—but I think now they are writing a new code, this one being some fifteen years old. And perhaps they will consider these new conditions. But here also comes another facer for the code—building without floors. The code also considers all these buildings that are built one on top of the other, like a layer cake, with little posts in between to hold the floors apart. Now that's cellular construction. In addition to these little pieces and fragments one related to the other, they also make little groups of cells. These little groups of cells are, in themselves, fire traps. And the fire trap has caused firemen a great deal of trouble and has probably burned up a good many citizens when fires break out. So the only thing they know is to construct ways and means within the cells by making more cells—cells which can be used in case of fire in connection with a group of cells. So you have to have a place where you can be protected on the inside and get through passages and corridors to outside stairs. That code again is probably applicable in three cases out of five, maybe four out of five, maybe four and a half out of five.

Then comes something never dreamed of by the makers of the code, a building with one floor, a great space with one floor winding up from the bottom to the top around it. So what happens? The condition is utterly changed. The code no longer applies. But they apply it and you have to figure out where the floor would be if it was a floor, and in that case provide exits to an outside stairway from each level as if it really existed. The same thing as the other thing.

So are all these codes made. I imagine you can take this idea of a code into the greater realm of law. Laws are very much the same. And of course it is impossible to make a law which will not come up against conditions for which it was never made and could not foresee. So what do we have to do in a democracy in order to prevent laws from committing murder? From murdering the thing they were designed to conserve, which is the chief, the paramount—human interest. Well it of course requires that the code be placed in the hands of men who have a conscience, of men who are to be depended upon to exercise judgment to prevent the code, when these emergencies arise, from doing more harm than good.

England has been very wise, and France, I think, has a similar wise institution—they call it the Appeals Court. When things like this arise and you take them to the Court of Appeals, the Court of Appeals "sits" upon them, as they say, and it's more or less literally true. And the Court comes to a decision concerning them. I thought New York had a Court of Appeals, but no. New York has what is called the Board of Appeals and Standards. Now an appeal and a standard—the very fact of making those two bedfellows would vitiate the appeal. But at any rate, it's not a court at all; it's just a Board of Appeals and Standards. It has been designed as a roadblock, so that people who try to get away from the code can be thrown back to where they may, or may not, belong. The Board of Standards and Appeals in New York City is only one of those things designed to be an extension of the rules and regulations of the city of New York and to deal with these discontents who come and say, "Well, this does not fit. This does not apply." But instead of having a democratic institution, you have an authoritarian one, and the thing that was designed to rule and benefit humanity becomes a cast iron imposition which cannot be dealt with anywhere by anybody, unless you are willing to compromise and do what has to be done to enable them to say that the code has been complied with.

The Chairman of the Board of Appeals, when we had made our "appeal" and I was about to step down, said, "Mr. Wright, why don't you design your building according to the code?" I said, "Yes, your Honor, what you mean really is a la mode." and I walked out. Now in that reply was a little stinger—I don't know whether he got it or not. To design your building "a la mode" means there is no progress possible in building, doesn't it. It means that you are tied down to the things that are being done in the way that they are being done, or else you are invalid. Invalid, you know, as a word means *invalid*. You are no longer valid when you are sick. You are an in-valid. So our Museum, so far as New York City is concerned, is an invalid.

(August 2, 1953)

The Mile High Skyscraper

The announcement that Frank Lloyd Wright had designed a mile-high skyscraper sent shock waves through the architectural community. Here was something that appeared to belong to the realm of science fiction, not practical engineering-architecture. But contrary to public skepticism, the Mile High was indeed designed to be built, and all of the materials and methods were actually available at the time it was designed.

Apprentice: Mr. Wright, we were wondering if you would discuss more in detail the Mile High skyscraper that you're working on for Chicago. We've had a lot of questions among ourselves and we just can't find an answer, and we'd like you to.

Well now, they've been fooling around with tall buildings long enough. Why don't they build a tall one? That's all. There's no reason why they shouldn't, you know. When the man—who was it invented the elevator?—nobody knows. I guess he's lost in perspective. But the man, when he invented the elevator, made the upended street, and when the street became upended, who should say where it should stop? Certainly not the science of building construction, because that tower you've seen drawn there would be as stable as the rock of ages. It would be practically permanent if it were made of steel and concrete, steel protected by the concrete. And it's entirely feasible because its like a wire rope. Now how long is a wire rope practicable? How long is a telegraph wire practicable? How long would you feel it could go without jeopardy? Indefinitely, wouldn't it? Practically indefinitely. So what limit to the range of the elevator?

I think the Mile High tower is very conservative. The only thing that could stand against it or would be a threat to it would be the overturn; the weight of it is nothing. And the overturn could be taken care of by the principle we've employed in the Johnson Tower and in the Price

Tower to a certain extent, and that is the taproot foundation. It came to me that that was the only practical foundation when I went through the forest here. We'd had a tornado. We'd had two of them as a matter of fact, and when you went through the path of the tornado you'd see most of the trees lying flat with their roots a vertical mass. They had overturned and the root mass had risen as a wall. But there were certain other trees standing still, bent over a little some of them, but still standing. And they were the trees with taproots. The root had gone down in, the pressure had been exerted upon them and bent them a little bit perhaps, but they were coming back and they'd soon be erect again. Well, there was the principle of the taproot foundation that we've employed since. And it's new somehow to engineering, I don't know why. But the elevator is not new to engineering, and I think there is nothing in the principle of that tower, the Mile High, that is not what you might say truly conservative.

Apprentice: Would it sway in the wind, Mr. Wright?

A little, not much. Not much because of its shape, you see it is 400 by 500 at the base, and does a church steeple sway in the wind? No, because the wind has no pressure on the top. That's why I made it the shape that it is. It's really a steeple with no wind pressure at the top. And as it comes down, even the shape of it defies wind pressure, because you notice that it's a tetrahedron in form. It's really a tripod. Now the tripod is the surest form of resistance against outside pressure from the side, because every pressure on every side is felt by the other side and resisted by them altogether as a ring. Well, that's true of this form of structure. From whichever direction the wind comes, the two sides stand braced against it. That's the nature of the form. Architecture dictates that in the nature of the thing lies its virtue and its use. Every individual employed by the state, and then some, could inhabit that tower, because I think inhabitation of 3,500 to 5,000 people wouldn't be much.

Now why build such a thing? Tall building is fascinating, has been, will always be. Towers have always been erected by human-kind; they seem to gratify humanity's ambition somehow, and they are beautiful and picturesque too. That's why they build church steeples. That's why the Gothic went up in the air. That's why all this has happened. And now that we have the means, why don't we go higher up in the air? You can see on the drawing on the wall in the drafting room the relation between what's the tallest building in the room, the Empire State Building, and the Eiffel Tower, and the rest of it compared to what we could easily do if we wanted to do it.

(August 19, 1956)

A Journey to Baghdad

Well, boys, we've had a long, long journey. And of course I've been very sentimental about this journey because when I was a chap, oh long before I was your age, I was enamored of Hashid, Aladdin and the wonderful lamp, Sinbad the Sailor, and scores of those tales of the Arabian Nights. Of course that was Baghdad to me. And Baghdad of course is there now, but not the Baghdad that I dreamed of then. So when this commission came from Baghdad I was astonished, delighted and puzzled. I didn't see how they got on to a renegade like myself, a rebel, but they did. And when I got there I found they knew all about my work—the engineers and the architects made a party in a garden and they were all there and filled it. Said it was the biggest meeting they'd ever had. I talked to them in a very unrestrained fashion, feeling free being way off there in Baghdad. They were very appreciative and they printed it, recorded it and printed it and distributed it all through Iraq. So I'm on record there and I don't know what the State Department is going to do about it; they'll probably do something. But not openly.

Let's stick to the last here, which is architecture. There is no architecture in Iraq, but what I was delighted to find when I was taken through the museum by His Excellency Assim is they have the greatest collection of Sumerian relics in the world. And the next best one is— where do you suppose—in Philadelphia! And when you see what the Sumerians invented, because they had to invent, you can't admire much what the Greeks modified later on, 3,500 years later. As a matter of fact the Sumerians were in on the first day of creation. There is no doubt, is there, that they were the origin not of the species but of the thing we call civilization. I always thought as a boy that it came from South America, the Isthmus, and from the Toltec region in Mexico. But there is no dispute now. I guess it goes back thousands of years previously to the Sumerians. Well, there is a purity and a vigor and a strength and a beauty in everything Sumerian. It makes what you see by the Greeks seem modernistic. And of course the Assyrians came later than Sumer, and the Assyrians preceded the Egyptians. From the Sumerian, the Assyrian, the Egyptian to the Greek—and the origin is there in Iraq.

The Garden of Eden was located at an old city named Edena, which was on the great canal taken from the Tigris and Euphrates. And that's about 120 miles, I guess, south of Baghdad. So we are calling this little island the king put his hand on and gave to me specifically, the Isle of Edena, and we are going to make a big feature of Adam and Eve when we do the building. Well, anyhow the trip was tedious, but comfortable enough. Amazing to think that you can cover all that ground and back again safely except for a doorman at the Dorchester House in London. The only thing we got on the trip that was any disfavor was a nick he gave me when he shut the car door on my leg before I got it in the car. That's something that he ought to be rewarded for, I suppose.

But here we are none the worse for wear, very much edified, doors open ahead of us for a new expression of old, old architecture. And there's where the shoe pinches now. Iraq's burst of prosperity, because it has more than two billion a year coming to it now in oil, no, a billion and a quarter a year, to spend. And of course it's an enormous sum of money, and seventy percent of it goes to the Improvement Board. We met the Improvement Board and they are all fine fellows. Quite up to their jobs. They have selected architects from the roster, practically, not so much I think because of what they can do but what they are reputed to be able to do. So a good deal of it has already gone. Corbusier is there doing a race track, no, not a race track, a stadium. And they've got Hilton in there to build a hotel. He's got his favorite architect building it, so the hotel is already merchandized and standardized to start with. I hope Corbu does better with the stadium—interesting to see what he will do. Then they have Aalto in there. They have a German architect whose name I don't remember. And a British concern has laid out the town, done the master plan of the city.

Flying over it I saw an island, unoccupied, practically in the heart of the city. And it was about two miles long and about a mile wide, maybe not so wide, three-quarters of a mile. And I wondered, well, when I came down and looked at the map there was that island with nothing on it whatever. And in figuring out where to build the opera house and develop the cultural center, I saw they had allocated the university on the ground opposite the island. And the island was a cleavage right between the city and the university. So I went after that island. And they said, "Oh no, Mr. Wright, we cannot, we assure you, do anything with the island. The island belongs to the imperial household."

When they took me to the king, I took the little map along with me, with the island showing on it, and after the first greetings I laid the thing out of the table, the desk, and explained to him what I wanted to do with the island. He listened very intelligently, and appreciatively too. I could see first he was interested in the Mile High. He wanted to know about that, and he wanted to know how much it cost, and I said we estimated it at about ninety million. "Why," he said, "that isn't much, is it." So I sent him the triptych of the Mile High as a gift, as a present, because of his interest in it. Well, he put his hand on this island place on the map and looked at me with an ingratiating smile and he said, "Mr. Wright, it is yours."

Now that converted me to monarchy right then. I thought here if culture can be presented to a man, open and intelligent and able like this to make it a reality, think of what we go through at home in a similar position with the Democrats and the Republicans and the House and the greedy architects all around, knocking one another to pieces. Here it would take fifteen years of pros and cons and jealousies and bickering and fighting to and fro to get possession of that site. And even then probably the legislators would get together and vote you couldn't use it.

Well, we've got it and we've got a great opportunity there in the drafting room now to demonstrate that we are not destructive, but constructive, where the original forces that built the civilization of the world are concerned. And we are not there to slap them in the face but to do honor to them according to our ability. That's the attitude I think that a modern architect should take toward the great life that's been his inheritance from the past and to which he pays scant respect. You don't respect a thing, as you know boys well enough, by imitating it. We are going to imitate nothing. But we're going to use the principles and the ideas that made Sumer originally a great force in human thought and feeling, and do what we can to carry it along.

(June 16, 1957)

Gammage Auditorium and Greek Orthodox Church

Apprentice: I have a question. I'm curious how you approach a particular design problem. Whether you work it all out in your head or what particular mechanics do you use?

Well, my dear boy, I don't know whether I work it out or the thing works itself out on me. But I never put anything down on paper until I have it pretty clear in mind. Now that's a little too much to expect of you youngsters, because that is a habit of a lifetime, a long time. And to see it definitely, correctly, imagine the thing completely, is no small feat.

But I have, we have, now three projects. One very gratifying, which I am glad to tell you about, is the one in Tempe for the University of Tempe. They are now a University instead of a college and they want a center, an opera combined with it, a double purpose house, three art galleries, with a center of communal interest binding the three together and a small theater. Now that's a very stimulating commission so far as I'm concerned, because my early training was all in the theater. I went to Adler and Sullivan when we were building the Auditorium building and then during the time that I had charge of the office, my end of it, there were two of us, Mueller and myself. He had the engineers, I had the planning and detailing end. There were thirty-two other buildings, theater buildings, went through the office and the old chief, as we used to call him, Adler, was famous all over the United States as an expert at acoustics. So I feel very well qualified to do this work for the Tempe College. Well, it was designed, it designed itself, quite naturally.

Well, then there's the Greek Church, which you will see coming pretty soon, coming in a beautiful point of land on a lake in California, near San Francisco. We are building on a steep bank. And in all these projects of course parking should start. You should start with the parking, not do the building and then try to find the parking, but get the parking and then do the building. That was true of everything I did for Baghdad. I solved the parking problem first, and it's not easy to do, and then built the building. Well, the same thing here in Tempe. We have an interesting parking problem, and then the buildings occur within the parking problem, and so it is with the Greek Church. The parking problem is most difficult of all because it is down in a ravine and the church is up on a side hill and so on. So it is a sort of a ratiocination in memory. But something of a challenge to your intelligence and your virtuosity always exists in the problem itself. Does that answer your question?

Apprentice: Somewhat.

I can't tell you how the wheels go round. I can't open the watch and show you. That's about what I would suggest that you do, all of you boys who are here with me. Cultivate your imaginations, get your project well in your mind, think of it, dream of it, turn it over lengthwise and crosswise, then go to paper. And don't start fudging on paper and then expect something to come looking at you out of the paper, out of the smudge on the paper. One of the first acquaintances of mine and the dearest friend perhaps I've had, was Cecil Corwin, and Cecil would start with the smudge on the paper, all over it, and then begin to rub out things. And the thing would come looking at him later on out of the smudge on the paper. I always thought that was the wrong end too, and I still believe so.

(December 14, 1958)

At Marin County, California

I suppose the Fellowship will be interested to know what happened at Marin County. Well, I was met by a couple of reporters and photographers—as usual, the photographs were very bad and so was the report. Then we went on to the meeting with the reporters at the hall in which the supervisors and I sat. Aaron *[Green, a former apprentice]* met us and took us out to the county, very beautiful drive through very wonderful country. There at the hall they had all the drawings up around the wall, very beautifully set and lit. You could really see them and they all looked very well. They sat me down at a table with twelve reporters and the supervisors. The reporters began, trying to look intelligent and ask intelligent questions, which they did occasionally, but not very often. The thing looked, to most people, I think, like a Roman aqueduct, but I had to tell them that they were not arches, they were pendant crescents, resembling arches, and then we were in deep water!

They went around from drawing to drawing and then they were appreciative and then they came and sat down. And the inquisition began! You could call it an inquest, I suppose, but a few of the reporters were really intelligent. I give you my word, it is extraordinary the material that gets into the run-around of the press. How little they know. But, of course, as you know, no outsider gets into architecture far enough to really know what the nature of it is.

We worked away at it for an hour or so. Then we were to go across to a hall, about a block away, and there the people had gathered to hear about the plans. Of course I assumed when I went to the hall that they had seen the plans. The hall was jam-packed with 650 to 700 localites, men and women. Two boys sat right down in front, and they were a very pretty sight. They were interested in architecture and they were only about ten or twelve years old! I began to try to tell them all about the thing, and I asked how many had seen the drawings. I asked them to raise their hands, and there were only two or three! So I said, "I do not see how I can talk to you about something that you know nothing about and have not seen. Why don't we adjourn and why don't you go over and look at the drawings and then come back. Then I will talk about the drawings you have seen." That seemed to be a pretty good idea, so up they all got, filed out and went across to the hall. And they jam-packed that so that hardly anyone could see anything. We had to wait for their return, and then they all came trotting back again.

"Now," I said, "I would tell you about the plans and the drawings, but it is not necessary if you have seen them, because you can judge for yourself. Which would you rather do? Just have me talk to you, as I would like to, or tell you about the plans?"

And one boy said, "Just talk to us the way you would like to talk to us, Mr. Wright." So I said, "All right," and I did. They were quite appreciative. Toward the end of the thing they got all wound up and everything became practically unanimous. There were no dissenting voices. The supervisors were all pleased, except the one unconscientious objector, who was not present, a Mr. Fusselman. Well named! And that was that. So we were practically accepted on sight. The supervisors called up the next morning to say that the Chamber of Commerce, which had been against the scheme from the beginning, was now enthusiastic and anxious to begin right away. I guess it is going to go ahead.

I think there never was a scheme evolved under such difficult circumstances. It had to grow, had to be flexible and was almost impossible at first thought, until we got this idea of making the one unit out of it, a growing unit, that could proceed from hill to hill. The drawings were very well presented, they were beautiful drawings. I think one of the best schemes we have ever turned out is Marin County. Of course, there were a lot of questions. They began to come close to the very nature of the thing, after they got a good idea of it, began to get hold of it, began to see the whole thing as an amazing simplicity, which it really is.

The drawings are now to go on to different places in Marin County and then leave Marin County and make a tour and come back. I guess all California will have seen it. The drawings will become a traveling exposition to continue for the next three weeks, and we will be getting our formal notice of acceptance within a week or so. So that's how architecture in California proceeds.

(March 30, 1958)

Last Things

Mrs. Wright: Would you, Frank, tell them about the picnic? Do you all know, do you all know about the picnic?

Boys, if it's to be terribly windy what do you say we give up the picnic? (voices: No-o-o.) We might find a place behind a big rock or something.

Brandoch Peters [Mr. Wright's grandson]: Furthermore your lamb has already departed.

Mrs. Wright: Our lamb.

Lamb? Roasted lamb. Vlado is going to look after it, he's the shashlik man.

William Evjue *[publisher]*: There's no wind out here now.

Not so much, it's going down. We're going to the Tonto again, and this time we're going to try to find that cave we used to go to. I don't think we went far enough last time.

Uncle Vlado *[Mrs. Wright's brother]*: Last Sunday there was nothing. I went through the whole Tonto Park. No cave.

Mrs. Wright: We were very comfortable in a big wind last time.

Well, it isn't a cave, it's just a hollow in the hill where the wind doesn't blow and where it's perfectly quiet and comfortable to sit. That's what we want. There's no real cave around there. Well, we leave here about five o'clock.

We'll go up where we went before, and maybe a little farther.

(March 22, 1959)

Mr. and Mrs. Wright at Sunday breakfast, Taliesin West, winter of 1954

Darwin D. Martin house, Buffalo, NY, 1904

Unity Temple, Oak Park, IL, 1904, skylight detail

Samuel Freeman house, Los Angeles, CA, 1923, corner window detail

S.C. Johnson and Son Administration Building, Racine, WI, 1936

Toufic Kalil house, Manchester, NH, 1955, typical Usonian Automatic

Marin County Civic Center, San Rafael, CA, 1957

The Last Picnic, Pinnacle Peak, AZ, Mr. and Mrs. Wright, March 22, 1959

THE WAYS OF THE WORLD

In Part Two we enter, more than through any other source, the mind and soul of Frank Lloyd Wright. Where Part One was autobiographical via externals, via buildings, projects, and the experiences revolving about those works, Part Two may best be described as internal autobiography.

Three principal factors contribute to the spirit alive in the following pages. For one thing Frank Lloyd Wright was a voracious reader. He *learned* from books, absorbed them into his being rather than simply reading them and putting them down. A prime favorite was Walt Whitman, and on Sunday evenings following our musical concerts he would frequently pick up *Leaves Of Grass* and read from it aloud to us. Raised in the Unitarian faith, he also felt a kinship with Transcendalists Ralph Waldo Emerson and Henry David Thoreau. Too, he was strongly influenced by the "writer-prophets," as he called them, including Dante, Nietzsche, Goethe, Unamuno, and particularly William Blake, whose mystical writings made Blake an almost living presence in his world.

Not only poets and philosophers but any and all gifted writers were grist for his development. O'Henry would make him laugh until the tears rolled down cheeks, and writers as diverse as James Thurber and H.L. Mencken were equally admired.

A second equally significant factor in shaping the interior world of Frank Lloyd Wright was one observed in 1929 by P.M. Cochius, president of a Dutch glass factory. While visiting the Wrights in Taliesin, seated in the beautiful Taliesin living room, he stared about for a moment, then said to Mrs. Wright: "This is the most beautiful room in the world. Your husband, Madame, is a great mystic." Then, in a very low voice, "But he doesn't know it!" Probably he did, for no one without mystic qualities could have said of a flower: "A flower is an intangible, maybe an eye looking out on us from the great inner sea of beauty, and precious beyond words for that reason."

A final shaping factor was his instinctive gift for seeing how all things are interrelated. He viewed all aspects of civilization as parts of a whole. Science was for him the capacity to take things apart, for comprehension. The arts put them back together, for understanding. And science and art were both subsumed under Nature, by which he meant those guiding principles that ennobled civilizations and men. In similar vein, architecture was for him the mother art, whose offspring included all of the arts: music, theater, painting, cinema, whatever lent itself to the highest expressions of men. His own work practised what he preached, for it integrated every relevant art form. He constantly maintained that a building was complete only when it blended design with engineering and included appropriate furnishing, landscaping, and all the details of decoration that made the work a total unity.

It is the all-absorbing reader, the mystic, and the cosmic integrator whom we encounter in the following pages. And we enter his vast and complex interior world by degrees. First we come upon tangible, practical observations, such as on raising children, on diet, and on money. Then we move to topics where perception and ideas add depth to observations, as in his comments on youth and age, on science versus art, on being human. Finally we enter the realm of intuition—or is it genius—where wisdom joins with observation and perception to examine Nature, essence, Christianity, the sum total of civilization.

"I have never wanted to be finished," he says near the close of this Part. "I have never wanted to feel that what I have done was the best I could do." Like the universe he integrated, his was a state of becoming to the end of his days.

OBSERVATIONS

On Raising Children

Apprentice: If you were bringing up a child or children at this time, what major influences would you submit them to?

Well, I think most frequently a good spanking. I think that is what they would deserve most and would do them the most good of any direction that you could give them. You can't reason with a child, and I'm quite sure that my mother's system was a good one. On the back porch of our cottage was a tub of cold water which was refreshed occasionally, and when I got in wrong and was unruly and unreasonable she used to take the clothes off me and souse me in that tub of cold water and the whole neighborhood could hear my yells. That is the way she punished me. Then she would rub me with a coarse towel and put me to bed to get warm and let me go out to play in about an hour. That's a punishment.

I think the parent's duty is to study, as in *The Mikado*: "My object all sublime, I shall achieve in time, to make the punishment fit the crime." That is the parent's duty, to make the punishment fit the crime. But not to spare the punishment. That old saying that we used to think was so cruel—when we got into this idea that every child has the right to a happy childhood—applies: Spare the rod and spoil the child. The rod doesn't necessarily mean a licking. The rod doesn't necessarily mean a whipping, it doesn't necessarily mean a cuffing. It may mean the taking away from the child, as the natural consequence of his act, what he has abused. But you have to teach the little devils that they're not all there is, you see. Because they don't know any better. They don't know there is anybody else. They don't even know their father and mother have any rights at all, and probably they haven't after they have a child. Probably nature intended that they should be retired and go into the background as soon as they had children. What do you think about that? Maybe the parents are only survivals after all, and should be treated by a higher up police force.

Apprentice: How would you develop them along the lines of a natural society and a natural way?

I think the first thing a child should do is to choose his ancestors with greatest care. He should do it very carefully, and with great foresight.

Apprentice: What conditions would you place the child in to promote this strength of spirit?

I would put him as much as possible on his own and give him all the things that would engage his imagination and attention. I'd like to waken him along lines of all sorts of love of his kind, love of beauty, love of his fellow man. And what would do that best I think would be a child's kindergarten. I think Froebel had the answer to a great deal of this. And I think all these others, Pestalozzi, and another Italian took this thing very seriously and went into it very deeply. I think Froebel used the greatest reason and was the greatest disciplinarian of all. For instance, he wouldn't let a child draw from nature. It was just a self-indulgence and a boondoggling. He wouldn't know anything about the thing, he'd fuss around on the surface to make pretty pretty pretty. Art has become mostly that, but it wouldn't have under Froebel. Because he said that before the child is allowed to run loose and free, he should know what it is that constitutes this beauty. What it is that makes these appearances beautiful to us. And so he took you into the realm of geometry and the child had to learn the basic forms and work with them until he began to see how they added up to all these various rhythms and things that you can play with after you know what is there, what they are. That was a pretty farsighted vision for an old German, wasn't it. And we haven't caught up with it yet.

You know, every moron likes to draw, if you let him just go and draw at something. But if you insist that he know what he is drawing, and how it got to be that way, and why it has these rhythms and why this appeal, then you are not talking to a moron any more. And when he gets that into his system, he has the key to a basis of design that will never desert him.

Apprentice: That is aesthetically. Now, how would you think a child should be brought up spiritually as a member of a natural society?

I believe that Emerson was right when he said, "Beauty is the highest and finest kind of morality." And what he meant was simple and obvious. If you are attuned, and you love sincerely, harmony, rhythm and what we call beauty, instinctively what is ugly will become offensive to you. And it will come in the realm of the spirit also. You will see how certain actions of your own are ugly, how certain others are beautiful. And growing up in you will come a sense of proportion in act, and a proportion all down the line that will make of you a democratic citizen in the aristocratic class even in spite of yourself. You may have a hard time with it, a hard time getting there. You may get chugged into cold water tubs, you may get this and that and the other thing on the way, but you will get it.

(January 30, 1955)

Women in the Arts

Apprentice: In such fields of art as writing and sculpture, and painting, women have excelled, but in architecture and music composition very few or no women really excelled. What do you think is the reason?

I've been asked that many times in my lifetime. Many times that question has been raised, why women do not have this projection, this projecting quality, this initiating that comes from, that would make them superior in the realm of creation. It is not so easily answered. But I think it is obvious that the more objective the expression becomes, the more it falls into the realm of the male, rather than the female, because the feminine nature is the receptive one, the conservative one. All the conservative elements in nature are feminine, belong to the female. She is the cup into which all this is brought in for the future, for the tomorrow. She conserves it, takes care of it and makes it, protects it. The male nature is the projecting nature, the nature out hunting, the nature fighting and struggling and bringing in the bacon and putting it on the doorstep for her. Well now, it isn't quite natural that she should be in that field so strongly as he.

There has been, according to nature, a division of activity, and a division of qualities. They complement each other, they are needed by each other, together they make one. No one is good alone. What would the one be without the other? But there is to me at least a division. Certain things are becoming to a woman that are not becoming to a man. And certain things are becoming to a man that are not becoming to a woman. And I think that is as natural as natural can be.

Possibly these qualities that are required in architecture and music are the same. You'll find that the mind of an architect and the mind of a great composer are just like this, because the composer is a builder. My father taught me to listen to a symphony as an edifice of sound. So when you listen to Beethoven you are listening to a builder. You are seeing him take a theme, a motif, and building with it. All sorts of imaginative differentiations and rhythms come out from his handling of that motif, and it is a source of continual admiration. You cannot help, when you finish listening to a Beethoven symphony, just knocking your head on the ground with admiration and respect for the way he can build. And what is building? Building is the same thing. It's taking a motif, a theme and constructing from it an edifice that is all consistent and organic—an organism as a whole. Now the architect's mind is engaged in precisely the same way as a musician's, isn't it. So if you listen to Beethoven handling a theme and get the secret of his interrelationships and interpenetrations of space, you are studying architecture. This is the reason, I think, why certain more objective, more projective elements, let's say, are basically male, and others are basically feminine.

Now of course when woman got to vote she wanted to be equal to man, and I think she has become less and less equal to man and more and more inferior to man when she tries to do what man did and wants to do what man does.

(January 30, 1955)

On Diet

One thing has occurred to me as we've been sitting here eating. The most valuable dictum on diet ever made, I think, was by the wisest woman probably who ever lived. Her name was Sarah Bernhardt. I suppose very few of you ever saw Sarah Bernhardt, the actress. She lived to a good ripe old age, and what she said was, "Eat what you want to eat when you want to eat it. But under no circumstances whatsoever eat all you want of it." Now that's the real secret of keeping your figure intact, keeping your spirits up, and really avoiding the doctor. Because it works this way. If you push back from the table before you finish and feed your instinctive appetite time after time that way, it begins to shrink. And if you eat less, you'll eat less and less and less and less. I don't think you'll ever get to the point where you won't want to eat at all, but at the same time, that's the way it works. Whereas if you eat a little more than you think you want, next time you'll eat just that much more and your appetite will swell. Her prescription shrinks your appetite. Very wise, and I've followed it. I always leave something on my plate, even if I'm hungry and would like to eat it. See, that's how I've preserved my girlish figure up to the age of 125. Well, that's the diet.

(February 1, 1959)

Clothing

You shouldn't give up a principle, and if there's a principle involved, then fight. But if there's no principle involved, and it's merely an idiosyncrasy that's at stake, give in. Let them have it. I'm sure that's good advice, but how to know where and when a principle is involved?

Well, there isn't much principle involved in a necktie. And if they don't like your tie, then you won't like it much. But this four-in-hand has always remained with me, though it looks like something that was intended to hang yourself by at the nearest lamp post. I never thought it was an artistic thing, and I don't think it is now. What do you think? That's why I don't often wear it. I think it's something that doesn't draw your features clear out, and you don't need that effect. But you all like it, don't you? Or did you ever give it any thought? Did you ever consider tieing your tie across under your face, or pulling it down from your chin, as though it were a streamer?

If you give much thought to our clothes and the way we dress, especially the way the women dress now, you're going to be very sad indeed. Because you're going to come out with absolutely nothing that has rhyme or reason. In my estimation the whole of society in our country needs a doctor. And not a chemical doctor, either, but a doctor of the spirit. Somebody who knows the nature of the thing done. Have you ever heard about the man who committed suicide and left a note saying that he was tired of all this buttoning and unbuttoning? If you'd start to analyze your clothing, you'd start to analyze this one bag for the arms, each, a bag for the body, a bag for each leg, one, two, three, four, five bags. It doesn't make sense, does it? I think of the Orientals, the Japanese for instance, a robe wrapped around and a girdle here, two or three thickness of robes for weather, and you loosen the belt and it all drops to the floor, and there you are as nature made you, no buttons. Nothing but undoing an *obi*, now that's Japanese. Chinese is almost as good. The Arab, similar—the Arabian won't wear the bags. It's only when you get into the realm of the British, and the French, I guess. Although the French never wore long trousers, they wore knee britches and silk stockings and buckles. I think they never wore pants. I believe that pants were invited by the British.

Any of you ever studied costume? It's architecture, isn't it. Well, the moment you begin on the modern, civilized costume of all the English speaking peoples, you'd better let it alone. You'd better go to the tailor and do what he says, because it is absurd. How many pieces make up the ordinary costume? A pair of shoes, two, a pair of socks, four, a pair of pants, six, and so on. Eight, ten, twelve, fourteen, multiplied by two, twenty-eight. That applies also to the houses people live in, and the way they live in them, doesn't it. Just about as much sense in houses. What's lacking, you see, is the study of nature. Now if we clothed ourselves according to the nature of our selves, our figures, and our shapes, we wouldn't be doing what we're doing now. You know what it takes to make a coat for a male now? With all the wadding in the shoulders, and the seams, and the lapels folded back, and buttonholes, and everything, and trying to shape it to a manly form, and padding out the deficiencies of the manly form, which is a sensible thing, of course. That proceeding you can't find fault with.

What is the term for these dressers in the lower categories, who pad the shoulders way out about four inches on each side, pull them in at the waist, and have great big floppy pants made small over the shoe? Who are those fellows?

Apprentice: They call them the zoot-suiters.

Yes, I've never forgotten a couple I saw on the vaudeville stage, doing a brother act, dancing with those big floppy trousers, and the big shoulders and the whole thing was . . . and we talk about the vanity of women! Good Lord! They must be entirely insensitive, because the vanity of woman is nothing compared to the vanity of man.

(October 12, 1958)

Socialized Medicine

Christopher Isherwood: I remember the first time an American dentist looked in my mouth, and he said, Ah yes, the ruined castles of England!

One of those sat right opposite to me, about the first time we got to England. He sat right opposite Mrs. Wright and myself, and talked about ruined castles of England! It was something terrific—he was terrible. Otherwise a very nice looking man, but his teeth! Well, medicine, socialized or otherwise will go on just about the same as the man in medicine. The idea of medicine that Dr. Bruckner has in Madison is that we die not of our ills but of our pills. And there are plenty of pills going around.

Pills are something else. I got a little note from Aldous Huxley and he said that the following had just come in too late to be included in his piece on *Brave New World.* In northern Italy the manufacturers are now feeding to their employees tranquilizers, and the tranquilizers, he said, would prevent strikes. And if there was any sign of discontent, in went the tranquilizers. And that they were also now no doubt blending with the tranquilizer a little aphrodisiac, so between the two they expected to have a very profitable season. Well, we can't settle the problems of England and America at the same time, nor of socialized medicine. I don't know what Dr. Joe Rorke would think of socialized medicine. Joe, what do you think of it?

Dr. Rorke: Probably it would be a hard pill to swallow.

I think we have socialized medicine anyway, don't we? Isn't medicine socialized before it is any use whatever to anybody?

Dr. Rorke: In a sense it is, Mr. Wright, yes. It's formalized, just like anything else, it's been stereotyped. That's the thing you have to fight against.

I think a doctor has to be very careful who he chooses for friends. Because an architect certainly is in that same position. Socialized architecture, boys, what would that be? It is, isn't it? That's what we've got. Socialized architecture.

(March 22, 1959)

Money

How many of you have studied into the nature of money, as money? Money is no more organic in character than the architecture we have rejected. If we look for anything organic in the nature of money, we would be horrified by the fact that it is merely a strong arm, and when the arm is tired and goes down, we have a depression. So if we are getting into the side of things that we call organic, that is to say, natural—looking into it rather than just looking at it—you will find money is a very interesting circumstance.

Of course, in itself it is nothing. It is merely a paper tool, and it could be anything besides paper, and it has been down the ages. You can use anything for money, provided something is there that gives money its value. And what is it that gives money its value, the only value it has?

Apprentice: I would say labor, Mr. Wright.

Well, no, that will not do because labor may be unenlightened, it may be merely slavery. But you are getting warm. The creative individual is the answer. The idea being that money becomes valuable because you can do something with it. If you take away all the creative individuals, all the men of ideas who have projected into the arena of our lives substantial contributions, money would not be worth anything. All you would have left would be a lot of vultures, living on money, who owned the money and tried to use the money, and their money would soon be worth nothing.

When it comes down to any real analysis of what you call money, that old adage, "Money is the root of all evil" is the bunk. It isn't. It is the use that is made of it that is the root of all evil. Wealth itself does not consist of money. It consists of the thing that has made money valuable, made money worth having, and keeps it worth having. Because you take the creative mind and the creative individuals away from society, and little by little society would shrivel and shrink. Even the vultures would not have pickings enough to make it worthwhile. Now who are vultures? The creative individuals being the only element in life that makes money worth having or worth anything, the vultures are those that gather it together for what it can do in itself. They have no creative mind in spending it. They are the vultures. The rich people are not necessarily the vultures. They may be the beneficiaries, legitimately, of men who really did produce value for money. So it gets to be a little bit difficult to classify. Anyway classifications are always bad, I believe, and organizations are liable to be worse than that. Who are the vultures? Who would be the ones that would fly around and, if the body lay there dead, would endeavor to sustain life by picking away at it, trying to find something worth eating?

Apprentice: The bankers.

Yes, they are part of it, the bankers. The speculators, the speculators in money, they are the vultures. The hoarders of money, they are the vultures. To hoard and to speculate is contrary to the very nature of the value of money. They are the ones who really destroy money. And the men who continue to make money valuable are those men of ideas, contributions, creativity, giving money something to do.

What would be the proper system? The system we have now is all on the side of the vulture. The system that we should have should be on the side of the creative individual. And the nearest thing we've ever had to it was called, at the time, social credit. The credit of the people themselves, as a body. The credit of the United States of America behind a piece of paper, not needing any gold or any deposit of any kind, except the will and character of the people themselves. That's all that made money worth having.

Now what have we got? We've got a strong-armed ring issuing money in their own name, virtually, in the name of the international banking system. They have created a purely fictitious thing in which you can speculate. Money has become a commodity. That is utterly wrong, isn't it, to have something become a commodity that only has value inasmuch as it is kept alive by creative endeavor. So architecture is not the only thing that is inorganic, up the wrong alley and a blind spot in our culture. Take money in along with it. And maybe if you did it, you would see that the capitalist system is up in the air, held up by this artificial money system, which it is. I am on record as saying I would like to see a real capitalistic system tried once, because I believe it would work.

(September 15, 1957)

INSIGHTS

Youth and Age

We can only work with the young forces, and the young faces, and the young in spirit. But it is possible for a young man in years to be quite old, in spirit. That old saying of Nicholas Murray Butler's is true: "Dead at thirty and buried at sixty." So much of that in our country—it's too bad. But I think most of my boys are young. If any of them grow very old, well I'd see something very unpleasant as a circumstance, and I'd get rid of it, I think. So they have to be young here. And I guess that so long as I can work with young people and see young faces, you the same, we'll both feel young ourselves.

I spent an evening once with my old comrades in Chicago—the old architects I used to know, some of them—at a dinner club of eighteen. And I was invited to spend the evening with them. And after the evening I went home and took off my clothes and got into bed and I thought I was sick! That's the way it affected me. I thought, "My God, am I one of them?" [At] the time I laid myself down—what is it?—laid myself down to die. It took me some time to get back on my feet again, just being in that aged atmosphere. And now I think there's no . . . nothing but a mental state. I don't see any reason why anybody should ever age; they can grow old in years, their faculties can diminish physically, but as they diminish physically they should increase spiritually. And there is a compensation there that should make elderly people, people of experience, more and more valuable as they grow older, instead of less and less so.

(October 22, 1950)

Teaching

How do you teach people? You tell them your experience, you tell them what you think. You can lay what you think is your experience on the table before them and let them pick it up if they can, or if they want to, but it doesn't very often work. So we don't get out of our present system cultivated individuals. We don't grow individualities. We develop personalities, and we carry personalities on to quite some extent. Some are colorful, some are interesting, some are dull, but rarely, out of the present system of education, do you get an individual development or, let's say, the development of an individual. Why is that so, do you think? What would you say was the matter, the trouble, the lack?

What happens to you when you get to college? You collegians ought to be able to tell—you've all been to college, most of you have. What happens to you when you go to college? What do you get? I guess the best thing is rubbing up against other personalities, and the frictions that develop naturally in a situation like that. You'd call that, perhaps, productive. It might be good so far as it goes, but it doesn't go very far. I think we get most quickly into the sphere of growth by way of action, and by finding out the truth about ourselves. There are mighty few boys and girls who want to know the truth about themselves, who would believe it if they heard it, or who would ever want to hear it again if they did hear it. We all live in a kind of illusory little world that we make for ourselves, and we seldom are able to see over the rim of that little world that we make for ourselves, either consciously or unconsciously.

Now when a group like ourselves gets together to work upon ourselves, that's really what we're here for. I wouldn't be so silly as to think that you could get an architect out of the average personality, because you can't. An architect is a builder, a constructor, a form-giver, and he's got to be a master of idea-giving, of ideas. He's got to know ideas when he sees or hears them. He's got to experiment lifelong in connection with those things which he himself has come to understand.

(June 18, 1950)

College Education

Ludd Spivey *[President of Florida Southern College]*: You must see that you have a much better opportunity of getting an education than if you went to some formal college where you would get a degree. Most boys and girls like to have the degree, but they don't want to work for it. They think that the symbol is going to get them somewhere.

You have said very well what I wish educators all over the country would say. Then we would probably be able to close the universities for ten years at least and reconsider. There is no doubt but that education has climbed high up in a tree, and is like a little boy down in Kentucky or somewhere, who climbed up in a tree to get a raccoon, got the 'coon, couldn't let go, and the neighborhood heard him hollering for help.

I think education would let go if it knew how. I don't think it knows how to let go. How could it? Most parents have children, sons and daughters, and so far as the education of the sons and daughters goes at home, why of course, it is very troublesome indeed, if it is there at all. So they have to be sent somewhere. And of course these schools and colleges are more or less creches, different stages of creches to which we send the boys and girls because we can't do anything else with them. It's too much trouble. Could anything be more troublesome than to try and provide for the real growth, education and development of the young human being. So education is more or less a refuge for shall we say the incompetent? Anyway, the colleges are doing a great work to relieve parents of their responsibilities. As such I dare say they earn their keep. But outside of that I don't know. I do not believe that out of that they are going to get the individual whom we want to see coming, believe we see coming.

You have heard it said here very often by all of us that you have been gifted with personality, you didn't have anything to do with it. You didn't shape your physical expression, and countenance. Your nose, eyes, ears and all that sort of thing were predetermined. Here you have it. Sometimes it is a gift, sometimes it is a curse. It depends on you, what you do with it. Now what you do with that involuntary gift per se is what constitutes your real individuality. You work it out for yourself. The word work in that connection is indispensible. You either work at it or it goes by default, and the animal side of your nature, which is your involuntary gift, takes precedence. You become more and more addicted to something or other, find more and more refuge in doing the conventional thing. Because it is easy to be conventional. There you surrender what we call individuality. To strive and maintain throughout your existence what we call individuality is hard work. It isn't easy. You incur all sorts of penalties, as things are now.

I believe with Dr. Spivey that all that could be changed by education. By a man like the Doctor, by entrepreneurs who would have faith in the individual rather than the mass product. But the mass product somehow in our country has been mistaken for democracy. When we speak of democracy we think of the mob. You've heard a lot about the common man. I never met one and I never expect to. Hope I won't. And as for a common woman, I hope she doesn't exist. That quality in the country that we inhabit was perceived as precious and indispensible by the forefathers who built our Constitution. And they built that Constitution under duress. They were up against it. They came here to be what they call free and they framed an instrument which probably is superior to anything, and of course unique in its time. It was a declaration in favor of the individual, his protection by way of a government where he as himself was inviolate. You can see now what has become of it. You now have conscription, you have all these anti things totally contrary to the spirit of the Constitution and perhaps also its letter.

Well I think education has done it. I think the colleges are responsible primarily for this perversion of the original feelings and ideas of the men who revolted from those conditions and came here to frame an instrument that would enable us to be free of them. As a matter of fact, the instrument has been amended and tampered with and turned about. And the independence of the states by way of the seventeenth amendment has been so taken away from us by federalism, by this idea that the world is one interpreted in the wrong way, that we have none of it left. (You boys are all conscripts. A conscript is a slave, you know, unless he's volunteered.) And that goes all down the line, until now we hardly know whether we are afoot or on horseback. That is all there is to it.

It is greatly refreshing, ought to be to you young spirits, to hear a talk as you just heard from Dr. Spivey. I think this college [Taliesin], so far as we know now, is unique. There is no other American college visible as the basis for a culture. Here we have architecture, which is basic. We can have no culture except as it has an architecture, and by beginning with an architecture which expresses this idea of freedom we have a living example of how freedom is not only possible, it is. So by way of this exemplar something has come to be which cannot be denied. You can see it, you can touch it, feel it, sense it, there it is.

I think America is the place where this sort of education is bound to be born for the people and by the people. We have sensed the lack, I think, in our country, the lack of a culture of our own, and the moment we see it, and feel it, we'll have it. One of the things I like about us, we

Americans, is that when we really are persuaded that is the thing we want, we'll get it. We'll get it fast.

(September 2, 1951)

Language

If you have "eccentric," why don't you have "in-centric"? "Centric, incentric, eccentric." The one being inside the centric and the other being outside the centric. So if they call you eccentric, it simply means that you're outside their center. You are on the periphery. You can give it a good many meanings, can't you? I was moved to it by the fact that I am editorialized in the local paper as the "leading eccentric of the region." I consider it a great compliment, but I don't know that they did when they wrote it. I think they were reproving me for being forty-five minutes late to a lecture, but I wasn't. I was only fifteen minutes late.

Anyhow the words we use we seldom understand the significance of, nor do we use them with any understanding. I suppose that's the origin of semantics. I don't know how many of you have been reading up on or studying semantics. It is really a very important study. Because when you get into semantics, probably three out of five of all the words you use you are using wrongly. I don't know of any word in the language that you can't see abused nearly every day by nearly everyone around you. How many of you could give a good definition of the word "character"? What would be one's character? And so it goes. "Beauty is but skin deep," is another misleading phrase—beauty in that sense, sense of the beautician's shop; all these words have been run ragged. And now that the advertising people have been using them, ad libitum, ad nauseum, there is no meaning left in any of them. The most noble words in the language apply to the meanest, poorest acts and features. "A beautiful sardine." "A lovely can." You can use it any way you please, and they do it, too.

So it's important, if you are a cultivated person and if you do aspire to culture, to be very careful how you use words. Brandoch [his grandson], at least, has learned one lesson so well that he catches me with it, and his grandmother. He has been taught never to say, concerning anything to eat, "I love that thing." You see, "I love this, I love that." He is starting on the right road. If you begin to think about the words that you use and the way that you use them, and save the good words, use them very carefully and very rarely, I think that is a good attribute of culture. If the word "love" is going to mean anything, you can't bandy it about. And if the word "character" is to retain its character or the word truth, or beauty, or any of those things, better use them very sparingly. There are plenty of commonplace, ordinary words for commonplace, ordinary things.

I suppose we have taken the beauty out of the word "God," too, by the way we swear. Every truck driver, and I myself, swear too readily. Then we begin to depreciate that word which is the supreme word, the God word in the English language. And after you have frittered that away, what have you got left? Not much, have you. You must have superlatives, and the tendency of human nature is to waste the superlatives. So we live a life of exploded, exploited superlatives. It is pretty nearly the same in everything else, too. You could find it in the realm of food, drink, smoking, eating—everything. So what is the lesson to be learned from the exploitation that is characteristic of this time, this age, everywhere. It has reached the point where nothing is really sacred, where nothing really means anything much. When you use the words all up, and there is no longer any real significance left in the language you use, what have you got?

I have always thought profanity was a kind of ventilation of emotion that had no other means of expression. That you swear instead of exploding. So you curse something, you see, you really curse the most beautiful thing you have in a moment of despair and anger in order to get relief. What is cursing, but that? Cursing is the burning up of something to satisfy your desperation of the moment and to give you momentary relief. Well, it is always a bad thing to indulge in. Expletives: you can use all the words in the language as expletives, just by the way you swear. And I have noticed many women, especially society women, who really have formed the habit of using every word they use as a sort of expletive, and by it I guess they get a kind of vicarious relief. They get an effect, they think, until it becomes so commonplace that it is just jargon and rattle. And most of it is jargon now in the movies. Unfortunately, or rather fortunately, we don't have television. If we had, you could see what these fellows do in language, what they do with the expletive.

It is the same in architecture. Many of these forms that have meaning and significance when we use them, are used by and large as expletives. They become eventually a kind of slang, even. Now slang is not necessarily expletive. Slang can be the growing pains, or the growth of the language. Because certain slang phrases, I dare say many of these fine words were slang once upon a time. A good slang phrase is really an artistic creation. But all slang isn't good slang. And I suppose that all this use of the expletive has its good side, perhaps. Too bad you can't keep the good side and throw away the surplus. But heated language, heated expressions if not designed and used for picturesque effect, are vicious. Because pretty soon the intemperance that they express and portray becomes characteristic. And you become intemperate. If you are intemperate in spirit and feeling, you are going to be intemperate in language, and when you become intemperate in language nobody is going to listen to you much. You will be like the buzzing of a bee in a dark room.

I think it is a good thing to keep a good rein on speech and not swear too often. I have noticed the tendency to swear, especially when you are hurt—at something which you stub your toe on, or hit your elbow, or get a knock on the head. The quickest tendency is to swear, isn't it. Well, that simply shows that something is being spilled from the inside that isn't too good. I suppose if you were hurt accidently, and you were really good inside, the tendency would be to pray! But there you have it, you see.

It runs through architecture just the same, through creative effort, through everything you do. Avoid the expletive. Avoid excess. Don't feel that because somebody has built a wall with a slant of two or three or four degrees that if you build one with slant of twenty-four, you are original, or that you are improving the situation. Because you aren't, necessarily. You are making a good thing an expletive, just like swearing—excess. Excess is always a sign of weakness. That is another thing to remember. Whenever you indulge in an excess of anything, in any way, in any direction, you are weak, can't hold it. You are a shallow cup, or you are a weak cup; and the weak cup breaks, and the shallow cup overflows readily and soon. Really strong men seldom swear. Really strong men seldom overflow on slight provocation. If a man is really strong, it takes a good deal to tip him over, to fill him up so full he runs over. So always as against every temptation, as against every tendency at the drawing board, always in reserve, keep something back—don't push the thing over the edge.

I suppose that is the origin of the term "conservation." But all these terms have become abused, and a mere lid sitter and a mere stand patter is a conservative! Well, now of course he isn't conservative. Very few so-called conservatives are truly conservative. They are obstructionists, they want to keep things as things are; they resist change; they want to see things right where they were when they left them, mentally, physically, and spiritually. And so they are impediments to progress which a conservative could never be. You know the word "radical" is one of the most beautiful in our language. And yet it has been perverted to mean chaotic, red. Radical means "of the root." Radical means "root." How it ever got to be that obstructionists could be called radicals is beyond me. It shows what I am talking about here now, how the language becomes perverted to mean exactly the opposite of what the meaning of the word is and should be. We think of radical as "red" and destructive, wanting to upset things; whereas, as a matter of fact, the radical wants to get at the meaning of things and preserve things according to their significance. He is the man who goes to the root to find out how that thing grew, what made it what it is, what it can do, what the nature of it is—that man is a radical.

(December 10, 1951)

Nature's Housing

This morning, boys, apropos of all this codifying, lawing, etc., etc., I wish to pass on to you a little lesson in housing which I have myself received. I'll try to show you what housing in nature amounts to—and if you really want to study housing, what a good place nature is to go and study it.

Given this cold dissector of life which we call science, it is science that seems likely to codify, crystallize and administer all of nature, and indeed all of our American life. Science derives rules of measurement from inanimate things. But the making of such rules or codes should not become a habit and should not be blindly obeyed. If the creation of a good form of free life for ourselves is our aim, such codes must freely be changed, as organic changes in life are bound to occur. Opportunity to function for the greatest good of the most deserving should be the end and aim of genuine democratic authority in order that quality may result. Only in light of that kind of interpretation of democracy is science useful or really successful. I believe, however, that science has, more by our own default than its own, so far overshot its humane value to us at the moment that we need "catch up" with the new tools which science has already put into our new tool box.

I do not think this catching up can be done if we depend upon the scientific mind, or upon the subjective mind we call taste. Something more is needed. Something is sadly missing in the way of knowledge of the spirit, which we do not seem to have. Or if we have it we do not really apply it. What that something is, is what we as architects would like to live to learn.

That something is just what we too, as architects, have missed. I should say that what is missing is greater art and a more profound religion. If the day ever dawns when science, art and religion become as one by recognizing each other's qualities as different but in reality reinforcing each other, then we would have something like this thing we are now missing.

Boys, look now carefully, critically, at these exquisite, infinitely varied little creature-houses which I have here under my hands—sea homes. *[Frank Lloyd Wright empties trays full of shells on the table.]* Here you see natural housing. Is it on a lower level than ours? Yes, in a sense, but isn't this humble work of this lower form of life which you see here a marvelous manifestation of the beauty of organic process? *[Spreads the shells apart in bewildering profusion on the polished wood table top. Fellowship gathers around to see.]*

Speaking of human housing, here are excellent lessons for young American architects. For instance, if the human mind is so limited that it can only take in the beauty and fitness of one special type of this species, we are deficient in appreciation and lack understanding. We must inform ourselves, if we really want to develop a culture of our own. That way we do not have to submit to these unnatural limitations by code or formula in our designs for our own houses. And we must not, in the name of science, submit to some official dictum intended to guide but really frustrating to our own human performance when we attempt to house ourselves.

Compare what is done here in the life work of these little nature creatures. See in the housing of this lowly life of the sea how natural housing is doing exactly the thing we seem to lack living in naturally inspired appropriate forms. The quality of invention here seems innate. In this varied collection of small houses, hundreds of natural beings built their own houses on principle, and every one of them is beautiful. Consistent variation in them is never finished. Creation of the beautiful is here seen going on and on, forever. No question of privilege or degree is here. All is a happy matter of work on natural design. Such multitudinous expression of design as they represent should indicate what "design" might mean to us, were we to be similarly inspired.

There is no good reason why our dwelling-places, the housing which we so stupidly perpetrate, is all alike all over this country. Why shouldn't our houses be as fertile and resourceful in design as we see here in these little sea-houses? Why do we ourselves need take any one expression of formula and stultified by our own stupidity carry it out to a dead end, execute it as though that were our all. Are we cashiered by our own cupidity? Here in this collection of little sea houses is an inspiring lesson. So study these little shells to see that all these little houses are doing the same thing to the same end. Also observe that they are not doing it in the same way. Nature's most beloved asset—individuality—asserts itself here and always succeeds. This clam shell, for instance, is based on the opening and shutting of the house: halves hinged. These others are without hinges. Are clams, being more mechanical and less ornamental, to be considered a higher development? Or being less mechanical and more ornamental, are these others superior?

You can see how all these significantly varied but concordant shapes, with their ornamental lines and designs, form textures and shapes obedient to sea forces exerted on their lives from within. Each shell has been thus "designed." Each pattern of ornamentation that we see is appropriate to life and environment. That is to say, the exquisite forms of the shells themselves are all the consequence of innate obedience to forces exerted upon their shell-ship from within, as the shell itself is formed.

Probably this particular small being [shows a coral filament] grew in a coral bed, where the very shape and every feature of the house was necessary to the preservation of its life under existing circumstances—for instance, keeping its inhabitant from being destroyed by alien forces. That is true, generally, of all these more highly developed cellular designs. What an extraordinary fantasy we have here, and all of it natural.

Here boys you see the true example of "Such as the life is, such is the form." Every single shell in its effects comes to its own conclusion, as an individual. However one may start or whatever the ultimate may be, every little home-maker has developed individuality. See this amazing variety of means sensible to remarkable ends. Now, when you get the secret governing the houses of these little things of the sea, you will have learned how a common principle persists the whole variety of nature's housing. Then you will have the secret of characterizing differences in housing on earth a sense of form that might apply to the human family if it were more aware of and respectful to nature. And you will command a true, inspiring dissidence.

See the utter differences harmoniously existing here between, say, these two little denizens of the sea? Yet what do both have in common? And here, in these longer, thicker ones are internally reinforced shells, a consistent structure due to scarcity of raw materials. Here, in this one, see the economical use of webs and the reinforcing-rib instead of the thicker, heavier wall mass of these other outer-wall-bearing constructions. Pattern is unique in each of them, seemingly predestined to anticipate purpose. Here are the children of movement, movements of the creature within and movements of the sea lashed by the winds, construction impelled by wave and tide in which it has grown. Why can't we be as rational and fertile in our housing? Why can't architects for human beings on earth be as sensible as these little creatures of the sea?

Look at this little house! And that one. And these others. Imagine! These are homes! This infinite variety is the expression of one idea. This inspired variety can go on forever, and does. Yes, it is infinite. That is why I show you these little manifestations as ideal housing.

Well, finally, what is this element in nature that produces, on principle, such fascinating, rich, harmonious, rational individualities? Isn't this expression the result of what we might call God in them? This could be. And it is the same element of individualism that produces the differences in human beings. Yes, it is all the same. The answer is clearly written in the great book of creation in which you may some day have a page of your own. Because there, in the principle of nature, is where the artist finds light shed on what he sees and feels.

As you see here, there is never a limit. Nothing indicates that the thing could end so long as the principle, inviolate, is in motion . . . . But nothing like this from the sea will come to us of the land until we too become similarly imbued with the nature-principle, and so sufficiently masters of our own lives to interpret that principle in the lives of others.

(March 21, 1953)

Science versus Art

When you compare things, you are on the surface, you see. You're superficial. You are learning only by trying to see what you see over here with what you see over there. But if you are really eager to learn and want to learn something, you look into that thing, not at it. The man who learns by comparison is only looking at things—and the man who learns by analysis is taking the thing apart and looking at it from inside. Does that explain it?

Apprentice: Yes, Mr. Wright. You also said that scientists can take things apart but cannot put them together again.

Science can take anything apart, and that's its office, but it never can put the thing together again to live, you see. Science can give life to nothing; science can only provide you with the constituent parts and to put them together again to live after its life has been taken is beyond not only science but even art. So we can't allow science to take the life of the thing that it takes apart. Let it take it apart, study it and tell us all about it.

And we'll be grateful and we may use it—I'm speaking, when I say "we," I mean creative artists. It's only the creative artist that has any living relationship to life. And of course art and religion are really the soul of a civilization—we call that our culture. Now a civilization like ours which amazes the world, and is amazing, as a civilization, has yet to know art and religion, too. This ideal we follow, we call it democratic, Declaration of Independence has no religion now—no real religion. We're using the old ones that were based upon a totally different kind of life. And as for art, well, we're not on speaking terms with it.

Architecture is our blind spot, as you've heard me say so often, and it's our office. It's going to be your contribution to society to become interpreters rather than dissectors and depictors and trying to patch things up, trying to get inside to see what the thing is like and come out with something as helpful and making it beautiful for what it is. Not trying to make something beautiful against its nature—superficially what you might do by comparison, but which you will never do by analysis. So the creative mind is a restless, inquiring mind, always looking at the thing and wondering what's in there, and how it got there, and what it's going to be, and what it's worth. Well, the scientific mind is not dissimilar in that respect. But the scientific mind is not the inspired mind and I'm talking about inspiration.

Here comes that old definition which I think we ought to put on the wall here somewhere I'm going to do it that old Welch Mabinogion, the triad, the wisdom that's come down, and these little sayings of three, King Arthur's Round Table. You've heard this, you all know it, the definition of a genius. Now a nation has a genius, a man may have a genius. Genius means the inner nature of the thing. Well, now, the definition of a genius that comes down from the ancient Welch: a genius is a man who has an eye to see nature. Now any comparison's out right at the start. There's a man who's looking into things. An eye, a kind of an eye, that can see nature. Next, a genius is a man with the heart to feel nature. Now, through that feeling for nature comes what we call inspiration love for nature. Then the last one is a genius is a man with the courage to follow nature. In other words, believing in what he sees, that's where he's going to be what he's going to do. And I think that's the best definition that I ever heard in fact the only one that comes anywhere near.

I never liked Carlyle's: a man who has the capacity of taking infinite pains. Well, of course, that he has. But, that doesn't define genius. But this does. The only thing that's needed to clear it up and make it complete is the definition of the term nature. Now, when we use nature in organic architecture we use it with a capital N. You write God with a capital G, most I mean, the world does. But I think it's a great mistake not to write nature with a capital N, because there is all the body of God that any of you are going to see Nature. And if you regard it in that sense, why you're already looking *into* instead of *at*.

(August 4, 1957)

Anarchy

I have never known what my real political complexion was. I have suspected myself of being what is called an anarchist, but I was never really quite sure until I have been reading here the thought and something of the deeds of the founder of American anarchy. And I find that this is really what I am, this is really what I believe. You see, the word anarchy has been like most other words, sold down the commercial river and made into a horror by people who own property and who are afraid of its being taken away from them. So an anarchist has got to mean a man who will kill, burn, destroy, tear down governments, murder women and little children.

Now here [points to book] you see all sorts of distressing topics like the origin of the national debt, for instance, which it isn't so pleasant to read about. Another topic that would be interesting was the revolution of 1688—the death of Charles II. This isn't the thing at all. Where is my little red book? It is the same shape and size. I guess the great liberals are all out of fashion, such as Edmund Burke. I'll tell you a little more about Josiah Warren, who was the first great anarchist.

Warren believed anarchy could be accomplished by way of equitable commerce, by building equity villages and actually performing. He would never proselytize. They could never get his feet on a platform. But if people would come around and sit with him, he would always talk to them. And he did his propaganda in that simple way, and by performance. He was greatly against talk, because he believed that if talk could be cut off from the human animal, a great many things would be possible that are now impossible just because we talk so much. That is the kind of man he was.

He founded stores upon the simple principle that a man who had anything to sell or had his labor to sell—which is really what he has and what he is—if he can dispose of it at what it costs, that is all he has any right to ask. That when you go beyond that what you have to sell costs you, then you're on dangerous ground and you're privateering. That is the exact opposite of the principle on which we now live and work. So he issued labor notes, and out at his store he would let you have any commodity that you desired, provided that you'd sign a note. If you were a plasterer, for example, to give him so many hours plastering. There was your currency. It was founded upon the actual ability of the individuals composing a neighborhood to produce. So instead of having a gold standard, he instituted the actuality of the labor standard. Well, of course that is anarchy. That is anarchy so far as our present system goes. And so it was in all these principles and things which he advocated. There was this element of basic simplicity, relating so called cost to actual value of performance. And so it went morally the same way. That thing to him was immoral which was founded upon the greed or covetousness.

Jesus was the great anarchist, and when he said the Kingdom of God is within you, he made the great, basic anarchic statement. If the Kingdom of God is within you, it is not a government. It is not anything outside of you. It is not anything men can come together and agree upon because they desire police protection or something of that sort. So this principle of anarchy and anarchism is profound. And it does lie at the root of all moral conduct, of all basic human life, regardless of its institutions. As Jesus himself said, he didn't want any institution—he didn't want a church, for instance. He refused to consider the possibility of churches or organizations. "Where the few are gathered together in my name, there is my church."

So it is with the principle of anarchy with Josiah Warren's principle in everything he did and everything he thought and the way he lived his life. He was an extremely ingenious man. And he was very fond of printing, because he believed that the thoughts which people talked out and talked about and talked over so much should be printed committed to the printed page. There they would be more effective, and people would have a little more reliability in their systems when they wrote than when they talked. I think that was a mistake. But he was a great printer, and he gave us the press which today is the whole press, that is to say, the cylinder press, which would do sixty-five impressions instead of six or seven a minute. Now when he did that, the man who didn't like talk put a stream of literature in the world that the world never saw the like of before. He was very ingenious and very courageous and truly individual.

Naturally the whole basis, the norm, of his society would be what? Not committees, not associations, not institutions, nothing of that sort. It would be simply and inevitably, the individual, as an individual. You see, anarchy is the great championship of the individual of his rights, of his responsibilities—which is the terrible part of it, you see. When you assume the rights of the individual, you cannot assume a right without a responsibility. And that's what he made so clear. That anarchism is the end of irresponsibility; it is the end of license.

Anarchy is the beginning of the era of strict individual responsibility. How different it is from the way that it is usually thought of! Well, the difficulty with it is the difficulty we have found with democracy. We can talk democracy and we haven't got it. And we aren't likely ever to get near it as we're going, because we haven't got the individual development necessary to assume the responsibilities that go with it. The great lesson that you learn from this little book that I have been reading is that, in true anarchy, there is no getting away from your individual responsibility—not only to yourself, but to everyone. Anarchy is also the capacity in yourself to allow that right to others, even though they differ from you. And it is this ability to hold your own at the same time that you allow other people to hold their own that constitutes the true individual.

You see how different that is from our concept of the party man. The party man to Josiah Warren would be the devil himself. Because there can be no party man when every man is determined that, in his own soul, every man shall have the same right that he has to his own opinion, to his own way of life, and all that. That is why the anarchistic faith is so far beyond the present circumstances. So far beyond the present circumstances that it is considered treason, even, to talk about it in the face of institutions. Because this faith in the individual would reduce all institutions to a mere coming together, as we do here, to pursue a common course and common cause in friendship and tolerance—each of the other. Now a high ideal of that sort has crucified a great many men, and I guess nearly all the great ones since time began have pursued that ideal in some form of policy.

Communism is the antithesis of anarchy. And of course, communism is for child-like individuals. And institutions are for incomplete personalities who have not arrived at individuality. No individuality, no anarchy, you see. So, if you would take count among those people that you know, who you would consider capable of this self-control, of this mastery over self and circumstance which constitutes the basis of the anarchistic faith, you would see how far away it is. But it is a great ideal to hold in your minds and hearts, especially if you are architects. If you are architects, you are basic, and all that is required of you is basic in character. You must have integrity, you must have quality as an individual, you must have this innate power, in some primitive form, that can become stronger and stronger.

(March 11, 1951)

The New Romantics

I wonder how many of the boys here, and the girls here, know the connotation of the word "romantic" in connection with architecture, or in connection with any artistic movement. It's always been greatly confused, you know. If you were a romantic, you were all sorts of an elaborate, unrelated, imaginative foolishness. You had no relation to reality. Romantic meant nothing, as a matter of fact, except somebody's peculiar taste.

Well, the romantic movement is anti-taste, believe it or not. The romantic movement attaches itself to such is the life, such is the thing. That is Coleridge, and from Coleridge it came down through Carlyle and through most of the poets of that day—they were romantics. And romantics connected with the inspiration of nature, the natural thing. Here we have the flower. Why does the flower flower? What is that element in nature that you see everywhere, blooming, striving for blooms, striving for blossoms, striving for what we would call beauty. So, to the romantic, beauty is a natural, and no substitute the way it was during the Renaissance, where men were merely aimed at by art to impress upon them some novelty or some experience that they couldn't understand if they wanted to.

So, reality and the romantic movement are now on speaking terms. I do not know how many of you have followed that, but it is a very interesting progress. And it has been a really very great battle all down the line.

When I first came out, after Louis Sullivan, with the term organic, that meant romantic in the sense that it was nature. It was rather difficult, at first, to connect the two because somehow a romantic was Oscar Wilde with a flower in his buttonhole, talking elaborate and witty nonsense. He was the bad angel of all that period, and of all that idea and movement. So it is very easy to get the thing inside out and upside down—this term romantic.

Of course every poet is a romantic poet. Even Whitman was a romantic and Emerson a romantic, *Moby Dick* romantic. So here we have architecture now, the last one to come in, and the battle has been pretty severe—is still going on. The struggle to free architecture from idiosyncrasy, to free it from the willful act of being governed by taste, anybody's taste.

Without knowledge and without nature study, and without going deeply into the circumstances of the time and the place and the man, and endeavoring to be appropriate to all these, you are not a romantic. Isn't that inconsistent with what idea you've had of a romantic person? You know what the figure is, ordinarily, that came down from the eighteenth century. Now we pass to the nineteenth century when it got confused. We are trying to get it clear in the twentieth. And if we do get it clear in the twentieth, we will have an organic architecture, architecture being the last. We have had it in literature, we have had it in music, but we have not had it in architecture.

Now we are having it and you, our children, are the romantic twentieth century in architecture. Do not belie your heritage. If they call you romantics, do not mind. It was not long ago that it was an epithet of disrespect, especially in England. "Oh, he's a romantic." And that removed him entirely from the category of common sense. Whereas, as a matter of fact, you had to get into the catagory of common sense in order to deserve the epithet. It is going to come up time and time again in your lives—you are going to have to fight that battle even now.

What is romance, anyway? Who has a good definition for romance in its true sense. Ever thought about it before? Of course you have. When I was in England that was the insult they hurled at me the most often when I was giving this Sulgrave Manor Board Lecture—that I was romantic. And that seemed to carry with it some opprobium where the established British taste was concerned. It was still a matter of taste!

What we want to do, as architects, is to put taste in its place. What would be the place into which taste could be put? Usefully and becomingly? Taste has been my ememy lifelong. I have been fighting people with taste ever since I could wield a pencil. And, let it be confessed, my own too! Because we all have taste and we all like the taste of certain things. The word says precisely what it means. You taste because you do not know. If you like the taste then you swallow it, not knowing very much about it, you just like the taste. It is good for you, more or less, or it is bad for you. It is more or less an acquired knowledge. Your instinct is all you need with taste, in order to like it or dislike it.

We are now emerging into a romantic period wherein nature study and knowledge of what is fit for what and why is coming up in architecture. It has not been uppermost in any of the other arts until the nineteenth century. It was not in the eighteenth. There were a few voices and a few individuals, all great ones, who insisted upon romance. Because romance is a flowering—it is this, you see—and this has a purpose and this has an origin and this has a scheme.

But it is not all as simple as that in the realm of the human spirit. Romance is the flowering of the spirit, the flowering of the soul of man, and not an excrescence. It is of the man, of the circumstance, of the nature and character of whatever is itself. Now, that is architecture today, and what a fight it has been to get it as far as it is.

(July 14, 1957)

This Sense of Self

What is it that we should be in possession of as a great instrument in this life of ours to develop, to subscribe to and increase by way of our own lives and by way of everything we do? What would it be? Wouldn't it be a greater harmony, a greater beauty of life, a greater becoming of everything that we are and everything that we do—in the sense that we see it all around us in nature, in a tree, in the rolling of the land, and the conformation of things we admire and we see in the qualities of light, and in this quality inside of us which is innate, which we call love, love of our neighbor, love of ourselves in the right sense. Because individuality grows and develops by way of love.

And love of self does not necessarily mean the self love in the sense that it is reprehensible in the Bible and reprehensible elsewhere. It is a high, fine quality which is to be cultivated and encouraged, this sense of self. Because when you have it, it's your business then to see that it is developed into a thing of beauty, that it is a concord, not a discord. And while dissidence may be essential to the development of that quality in yourself, it's not necessarily dissonance or discord. It may be different because you see differently. And we want variety in human nature, because you'll find nature very jealous of this thing you call variety. She makes a species and then tries to find ways of differentiating that species. She wouldn't be satisfied with one flower—a sunflower, would she? A helianthus? No. The whole gamut of human perception and everything we can appreciate and see is satisfied beyond words by just that single mere instance of what is capable or common to nature.

Now I believe that in the nature of the spirit, in the realm of the spirit, let us say, nature is hungry. What we call man, in himself as an idea no doubt divine, subsists, craves, develops and desires that same variety of expression. It's not necessary for one person to believe as another person believes. Our whole establishment of democracy was erected otherwise. It was erected on behalf of the individual, upon what is truly individuality—the growth within of the person, whoever *[he]* or whoever she may be—to the stage where you can say truly there is an individual. Now that I am certain is concretely, innately nature's aim.

So don't resist it and don't be too cocky about it either, because it's something beyond you perhaps and beyond your control, maybe. That I doubt. But anyway individuality, the individuality of the small town, the village as such, many villages, no big cities, no great trampling of the herd because the soul cannot exist in it—the soul exists only by way of individual variety, individual quality and character. And don't be foolish about it. Don't try to beat it before you are able. Don't be foolishly self assertive and what they call ignorantly arrogant. But for God's sake do be yourselves, quietly and with feeling and with a certain reverence for that thing which was given to you as yourself.

(September 20, 1953)

On Being Human

What you want to learn about boys and girls is about yourselves— what you are, who you are, what's the matter with you, what you might be. Sounds selfish, doesn't it? Sounds self centered; it seems to be a crime. Believe me if you're not self-centered, you haven't got any center. You're without a center. But the only center you're ever going to know is what is in your own soul. And if that center does not coincide with the great center, and you're not revolving parallel with that, you're going to be miserable, you're going to be in darkness. The light isn't going to shine for you. You're going to be always puzzled, mad about something, and in the end failures.

This sounds very moral but it isn't. I guess what I've been saying all through here would be considered amoral, wouldn't it? At least, it's not conformist. That's one virtue it has. And it is interior, which is another virtue it has. It declares to you by way of my own experience that nothing is lying around loose outside of you that you can't pick up—except to run with and have it taken away from you, or get into jail with it because it isn't yours. You can't pick up anything and keep it that isn't yours. You can't even see anything clearly that isn't yours. And all you can ever absorb or appreciate of any sort is what you have already in your soul. Now as you have it, you will find it—it will grow until it becomes operative and it becomes visible in you. But it's all there inside now and it's all waiting to be developed. And nobody can develop it for you. Nobody's going to do this for you outside of yourselves. It's only as you compare, experience, learn, by way of exercise of this light that's within you, that you'll ever grow into anything worthwhile. That you'll ever become architects, that you'll ever become anything else.

What's greater than being an architect? What is the greatest thing you can be?

Apprentice: A human being.

Humanity begins where the animal leaves off. You know that. We all have pretty much the same animal heritage. We get here by the same road; we have the same experience the same things happen to us, and we have what we call appetites, and we have this and we have that. But comes along that spark within us—I think it's light, a spark of light—which enables us to sometimes see. And that's where humanity begins, with that seeing something, by way of this spark which is transmitted from generation to generation. And that's what we call humanity. As you see more and more you become more and more humane. And you are able to do more and more with the spirit, with things of the spirit. But up to that time, you're just animals. You may be good ones, you have to be good ones. I don't think you can be a weak animal and be a great spirit. Because you'll be pestered, delayed, set back, put to bed, inoperative, if you're not good animals. So that should have your fond attention early, and you should conform. But who wants to stay on the level on an animal, die the life of an animal, and be buried as one? No one human.

When we speak of humanity we mean a quality, and it is interior. It is a quality of light that proceeds from the light of the world, the light of the universe, light as it is. And according to that light, you grow as a son of well, I think they call it God, but I never knew exactly why. That's a good name for it, maybe. But I don't think it's outside of your selves, a mystery that some day you're going to inherit. I think that all you'll see of it, you've got right now. And the thing for you to do is to look, listen and conform to that. It's the only conformity I would suggest to you. It's different for each of you. It's different for us all. It wouldn't be the same for me; it wouldn't be the same for Olgivanna; it wouldn't be the same for Tom; it wouldn't be the same for David; it wouldn't be the same for anybody. Except that it is one, it is the light, and as you are respectful, cognizant, obedient, in a way you grow. You grow stronger in spirit.

Stronger in spirit is the only strength that this country, or any country, or any man, needs. There is enough physical strength, God knows, on earth. And the machine has augmented our spiritual strength. And today by way of scientific invention we can do a hundred to one anything man ever did, but how about *him?* Meantime what's happened to him? What's he got? What has he gained? Is *he* any stronger? Is he any more competent to beautify his life—and no man can beautify his own life without beautifying the life of others. If you think that you can get away with it by something that you do for yourself, you've got to guess again, because it won't work.

Instinctively and naturally if you beautify your own life, you beautify the life of everybody around you. Just as that flower there in itself is having a happy time, realizing a principle, no doubt. But we share it, we get from it, it belongs to us as we see it. To the extent that we take it in, we are that thing. And so it is when you do this thing for yourselves, and become your self's expression, make your self an expression of this light within we call the spirit, just so long are you beneficial to human kind. If they can say, "Well, he's a great human being." no greater compliment can be paid you.

In architecture we want a humane architecture. We don't want buildings that simply say things by rhyme or without reason, nor by rhyme and reason even, without a soul. We want the thing to be extremely humane, of the spirit. From man to man according to man's higher nature, and that higher nature is never exterior. That higher nature is ever inside. And when we say that the reality of the building consists of the space within to be lived in, don't you see that philosophically we have abandoned all exterior thought, idea that anything outside it matters. It all must come from within. That is what gives charm and grace and beauty and integrity to the buildings that we build. And the more you can strengthen that in your own natures, the more of a break you give it, the more respect you pay to it, the more powerful you will be in making things beautiful. The principle will always be there and always working according to what you are yourselves, what you've got, how far you've come.

(April 15, 1956)

A HIGHER WISDOM

Nature

When you pursue any line of endeavor that is in connection with the spirit, what really matters is never easy to get. It's never on the surface, it's never to be looked at and found. It's only found if you look into the Nature of the thing, look into the character of what makes it what it is. And what is that thing that makes it what it is? That's the essence, the Nature of the thing. Well let's say that it's the nature of the Nature of the thing. Wouldn't that be it? To come back always squarely for any view or solution of a problem of the sort to Nature.

How many of you understand the way we're using that term Nature now, with a capital N on it? Do any of you not understand it? I'd really like to know, because it's important. It's where you have to start now philosophically in connection with an organic architecture. You have to start with a knowledge of what constitutes Nature, the nature of Nature. And it's not easy, I guess, to come by. How many of you have any doubts about it, or are confused concerning it? I'd like to explain it clearly, make it clear. It's not the common definition of Nature, and I think it's been sadly confused by the current use of the term, hasn't it. How many understand that Nature is the essential character of whatever is. It's something you'll find by looking not at, but in, always in. It's always inside the thing, and it makes the outside. And some day when you get sufficiently proficient in understanding the use of the term, you can tell by the outside pretty much what's inside.

But you have to go through all this to get it, and to be able to do that thing. When you get there they may call you prophetic. And they may call you lots of other names that aren't so pleasant. Probably they will. But everything that's ever going to be of use to you in architecture or in life or anywhere you go or whatever you do is going to be Nature, in some of its immensely varied forms. So varied that there's no end to the variety imaginable. Who could imagine a single variety of anything as a finish, as an end to that thing? It's impossible, you can't. All the variety and variation can go on forever, and I guess does—our forever. But what would our forever be?

(September 7, 1958)

Nature and Idea

The first step in nature study is what is the nature of this thing as it lies here unsolved. Then you begin to take it apart, begin to see what this is, what that is. Gradually you see why this is separated, why it hasn't come together. But you haven't got quite the way it should come together. What will coordinate all these things?

An idea is inevitably a coordination. It is a coming together of something that is separate or disorganized or incomplete. With an idea you begin to feel into the nature of that incompleteness. Why is it incomplete? What's lacking here? What is harmony, what is harmonious in this instance?

Now comes your drain upon nature, upon your knowledge of nature. You see the thing as it is, and more or less the truth of that thing begins to come to you. And not very long after that inevitably a vision arises in your mind. You begin to see something you haven't seen before and you try it out, put it together, see if it works. You may think you've got it, and you haven't got it that first go-off. The thing that seemed so good when you gave it a trial is not so good. But you see why. A second try will get you a little nearer to it, and by persistence and experience and concentration the thing will begin to come out to you. What is natural to that thing. What is the nature of it. And you will see that aspect of it as clearly as you see that palm tree over there, as you see these shrubs, as you see anything. Then it begins to take on its entity.

That's the process, but that's not the source of the idea. Where that lies, I don't know. Except that I do know that it lies in this thing we call nature. It does lie in this thing we call the body of the idea. It is way above us and is essential to us and of which we are an expression, imperfect, always in a state of becoming. Who knows what we're going to be a thousand years from now, even a hundred years from now. We're going somewhere, and in the going lies these varieties, lies these things that come together, that click, that make something happen that never happened before. That's not the idea, that is the working of the idea and it is the way it comes to you.

I don't think ideas are brainstorms, I don't think ideas are freaks, or happenstances. I think they're just as organic as all the rest of life. And I think it is the organic nature of all that matters. It gives you the power that you have. I don't think any of you will have any real power, except as you are natural, except as you belong to the thing that you do and the thing that you do belongs to you. Now you can dance all around it, you can cut figure-eights, figure-threes, and do the Dutch-roll backward, and you can be an expert, you can be a mountain climber or a trapeze swinger and be very showy, and still be no good at all where the idea is concerned. That's mostly what we get because we don't get back to the origin of whatever is organic and natural to the circumstances. Novelty is not it. Sensationalism is not it. The fact that you are arrested by something curious or beautiful is not it. The whole thing is extremely quiet when it is organic. It's simple, to the point, always. It isn't something you've invented, it's only something you've perceived. And it isn't yours to keep. That's my conclusion.

I don't think anything I ever had was mine to keep. It was merely something that I was to pass on, that I had to share. By doing it, I gave it. That's all. That didn't make it mine. And I think that's true of any idea. No man owns an idea. The greatest idea I know of is what Jesus said: "The Kingdom of God is within you." That was against everything that existed when He lived. Unfortunately the Christian religion got busy and made it inconsistent with everything that ever happened afterward, except the Declaration of Independence in the United States. And men like Walt Whitman, men like Emerson, Dante, all the great poets, Shakespeare, any great man you can name, they're the only ones who could understand.

(December 30, 1956)

Idea and Essence

Every idea that is a true idea has a form, and is capable of many forms. The variety of forms of which it is capable determines the value of the idea. So by way of ideas, and your mastery of them in relation to what you are doing, will come your value as an architect to your society and future. That's where you go to school. You can't get it in a university, you can't get it here, you can't get it anywhere except as you love it, love the feeling of it, desire it and pursue it. And it doesn't come when you're very young, I think. I believe it comes faster with each experience. One genuine experience, and the next is very simple, or more simple, until it becomes quite natural to you to become master of the idea you would express. We call that process of expression "design," don't we. What makes a good designer, a master of design? He's usually a master of the idea, he's usually a man of ideas.

Now all things that look like ideas, aren't necessarily Ideas, with a capital I. They may be very little things, and then we call them notions. The notion and the idea have to be differentiated. All of us are full of notions. Not many of us have ideas. But most of us really should cultivate, if we don't have it, respect for the idea. What I've been talking about here all of the time is the idea of the thing. The idea of the thing is the essence of the thing. And my difference between the common man and the uncommon man is the man who can see, love, and respect the idea. In other words, the man of vision. He's your uncommon man, and your common man is the one who takes it for granted and hasn't the disposition nor the mentality to penetrate the idea.

(September 7, 1958)

Jesus As Architect

The original promulgator of an organic architecture, you can say with truth, was that carpenter back there in Nazareth. The carpenter in those days was an architect, wasn't he. Jesus was an architect, I believe. He thought as an architect would think. If an architect were the prophet of organic architecture he would have said and acted and believed precisely as Jesus preached His own word. But not His disciples, His disciples queered him. They just got the thing all twisted and mixed, and so we have what we call the church and we have what we call Christianity. Very far from the teachings and feelings of Jesus. He thought that the Kingdom of God was at hand, if you remember. He thought it was just around the corner and believed in it so implicitly himself that he couldn't imagine it would not prevail tomorrow. If not tomorrow, certainly the day after. He believed this two thousand years ago, and he's speaking to those individuals today even as he did then. But how much nearer is the Kingdom of God today than it was in his time? Sir Alfred Wallace, the greatest English moralist who ever lived, and a very fine individual himself, died with the statement on his lips that man has made no moral progress since the days of Jesus.

So much did Jesus hope that the Kingdom of God was around the corner, tomorrow or the day after, that the number of people who have had the inner illumination that came to Jesus were enough to save the world from destruction. His teaching must have had great power, because they couldn't kill it off. They couldn't kill off Buddha's ideas either, nor Mohammed, nor Moses. They still live, in spite of all the hell and horror that has gone on in the world for thousands of years.

You know, I rather think that's what is the matter: they can't kill them off, and they can't make them go. Well, there's no doubt that great souls and great people have always lived great lives and have died the right kind of deaths. But at Jesus' time, when life was more difficult, a more personal struggle, the thing rose higher. As you take the struggle out of it, the farther away you come from the realization of the things Jesus preached, and loved, and would have had come to pass in human life.

So it comes down to this, that the fine thing, humanly speaking, is never easy. It's not something you can get by wishing for it. It's not something that will come to you just because you want it. There is only one royal road to getting things of the spirit out of the animal. That is to take a good grip on the animal, mortify the animal, and get this other thing by hard work on yourself. It is a hard road, but fortunately the harder the road the sooner, probably, you will arrive. Anyway, that is what Jesus preached.

Then see what they do with that preaching. Take Christian Science, for instance. Christian Science is in itself a very clean and simple sort of thing. The Catholic religion would be the same. They both make this thing easy. You just lay your burdens on the Lord, or confess to the priest, and any transgressions you have may be washed clean. By putting your little contribution into the box, you are paying for your transgressions. You can more or less in that way either wheedle or buy your way into Heaven. But it isn't like that, you know. I don't believe you can get there that way. And that applies to architecture as it does to the other things in life.

You have to suffer, you have to work hard for anything that you are going to have in your head. It is a great shame—I don't know why it is so—that you have to struggle, and suffer, and sweat, toil, and be thrown down and beaten for your lofty and high ambitions. There's some good reason for it. You figure it out. You'll have to. Maybe it isn't a good thing to know. Little Johnnie wasn't so very smart, either. He had the same yen to know where the sound came from when he beat the drum. And what did little Johnnie do? He cut out the head of the drum to see where the sound came from. Did he see? He did not. Now, the wise man doesn't cut out the head of the drum to know where the sound comes from, because he has a hunch where it comes from. You can't make him enough of a scientist to do that foolish act. So at least architects don't cut out the head of the drum to know where the sound comes from. They have that advantage over the scientist.

Which leaves the question just about where we started as always must be the case. One beautiful thing about it all, and that is that nobody can solve it for you. You know how Jesus' disciples all clamored for miracles, and they bored Jesus stiff. He didn't want to do them. Every time they asked for a miracle, He felt ashamed of them and tried to get away from them, but they insisted upon it to make their work easier. Then they could get the crowd, they could get the populace into the faith that they wanted to promulgate. So occasionally Jesus would perform a miracle. But He knew it was cheap, He knew it was dangerous, and probably those miracles have done more harm to the cause of humanity than anything else that's happened.

(June 4, 1950)

Ethics and Morality

What is ethical is the principle of the thing, and what is moral is only our endeavor to practise that principle. It may be the best we know, and we're doing our best with it, but morality can't be compared with the ethical, with principle. Because it's a man made custom, it's a man made habituation of what's right. It often, as you will find as you read your histories, has gone so far wrong that it becomes almost fantastically wrong. So stick to principle, which never changes. And shun the moral, that is, not shun it, but scan it. Scan the moral and see how it jibes with what is the principle which it endeavors to express and enforce.

Your moral man may be a really very bad man. A moral society can be a very cruel and terrible society, as indeed, if you remember the witches burned at the stake at Salem and the terrible waves of morality that swept over Medieval Europe and decimated the best people alive at the time. Well, all that was moral, not ethical. Ethics have never yet done anybody harm, except the crook and the pretender and the faker. The faker is up against something pretty solid when he's up against the ethical principle of anything. And I'm afraid the United States today, if it were to be stood up against the ethical principles involved in its conduct, would seem pretty terrible.

(September 7, 1958)

Civilization and Culture

A culture, a civilization is just a way of life, and there have been hundreds of them, thousands of them in the world. But a culture is the way of making that life beautiful, and that we haven't got. We've never even started on that road in our country. Who was that French guy that flung it at us. I have quoted him God knows how many times, because he was right that we were the only great civilization which proceeded directly from barbarism to degeneracy with no culture of our own in between. Cocteau? No it wouldn't be him.

Charles Laughton: No, I've heard it before but I can't remember who it is.

Anyway there is where we are. We are there because of too much Greek, of too much materialism in all ways, in all directions, but not enough of the spirit. Well, now, architecture is a profoundly spiritual qualification. That isn't very definitely put, but architecture is the basis of a culture, without environment and without a reflection of yourself as God-like in your environment. You have no culture. Architecture is the way of making that way of life beautiful. And we know nothing about it. Architecture is our blind spot. And when you go to be educated, you go up against a pile of rubbish, and you paw around in that scrap heap, pile of rubbish, and come out with nothing. And then they call you self-educated. Then you've been to college and you come forth an educated man.

Well, I don't call any man educated who doesn't know the difference between a poor building and a good one, who doesn't know the difference between harmonious arrangements that fit and belong and those which are not. How are you going to call him educated? He is at loose in society, as a menace to society. He makes the world more ugly. It is the uglier for having known him, and not the more beautiful—not a nicer place to live in because he lived. And while as Heraclitus said "all is change, and in a state of change," it is the center line of that change that we should learn how to preserve. That line of continuity that passes from here to there, from yesterday to today. And that center line would be a philosophy, and that philosophy to me is this more fluent philosophy of the East rather than anything the West has turned out.

Now that is a flat confession which need not have been made. All comparisons are odious. We've done the best we could, we in the West, and we haven't got anywhere with it to speak of. If you judge us by our colleges, if you judge us by our education, if you judge us by our buildings, if you judge us by our works of art, we haven't got anywhere yet.

It's time we did something, and we can't do much until we get the center-line fixed, until we know where that center-line is and in what direction it is going. That ought to be the first purpose, the first act of an education where a young man is concerned. And if he doesn't get that, he is at loose ends all the rest of his life. He'll be reading this and that and liking it and reading something else and liking that, being confused and futile and non-serviceable all his life.

Charles Laughton: I think that is the best definition of truth I have ever heard in my life—the center-line between change. I think that is a magnificent definition of it.

They stoned Heraclitus in the streets of Athens for a fool for declaring it, and that was because he was not Greek. He gave the lie to the whole Greek set-up, and that's why they stoned him in the streets of Athens for a fool. He declared, Heraclitus, that the only knowledge man could possess as man, as himself, was that all was in a state of becoming, all was in a state of change, and that the truth he faced was that what was fixed today would not be so tomorrow.

And yet, the hopeful thing and the great thing in his message was that the process of becoming was also perfecting, developing, growing inevitably, and that nothing could stop it. There was that pervading determination of direction on the part of nature which man might very well trust, and which he might give himself to with all his heart.

Now that to me is the worship of God, the only worship we can render. That's the only fealty, the only loyalty which you as young souls and young lives can be capable of. That is why sincerity is such a high quality of the mind and why decision is such a high quality of the will . . . .

To sum up, culture is a way of making that way of life which is a civilization beautiful. Making it beautiful is of course our concern, and the concern that is really living. The rest is makeshift until this thing enters into it. Then you have something which lives, and something which will always live because it is what lives today in all these civilizations that have disappeared. Their way of life is gone, but the beauty created by the artists of that time, their buildings, their sculpture, their paintings, whatever they had that gave beauty to the life they lived—we have it, and it lives for us still.

(January 18, 1953)

"For soul is form and doth the body make."
Edmund Spenser

Frank Lloyd Wright, 1877

Frank Lloyd Wright, 1887

Frank Lloyd Wright, 1903

Frank Lloyd Wright, 1910

Frank Lloyd Wright, 1919

Frank Lloyd Wright, 1931

Frank Lloyd Wright, 1945

Frank Lloyd Wright, 1954, (John Engstead)

AT HOME AND ABROAD

Part One examined the life of Frank Lloyd Wright as measured out by masterpieces; Part Two explored that life from within, explored the mind, heart and soul forged to fashion those masterpieces. In Part Three we find Frank Lloyd Wright surveying the world around him, standing fixed at the center of twentieth century American democracy, that noble experiment still in the throes of growing pains. As such, its faults seemed glaring to an impatient optimist like Mr. Wright. The root problem, it seemed to him, was "the new mass man," sprung of the population explosion of the early twentieth century. The net effect, he felt, was the ruination of the democratic ideal by what he called the mobocracy. He could be scathing on the subject of mobocracy with regard to American politics, crass commercialization, and the seeming degeneration of our total culture.

Despite the harshness of his rhetoric, however, his was never simply a negative view. Although he saw his hopes dashed time and again, his optimism kept rising to the surface. Like Walt Whitman he believed that "The cure for the ills of democracy is more democracy," a remark he quoted frequently. Like Whitman he too suggested a cure: "I believe the solution lies in each individual through the standards he holds, that it lies not in the political parties or radical movements but in human values and gradual trends from within, not in a greater complication but in a greater simplicity of life."

Finally, like Whitman, he offered a testament of faith. "They say that a prophet is without honor in his own country. Well, I doubt that. Otherwise how have I built some 759 buildings with my own hands. What other country could that happen in? None in the world."

As an American architect Frank Lloyd Wright deplored the fact that American cities remained Medieval anachronisms, dating from the time when men banded together behind high stone walls to seek protection from their fellows behind other high stone walls. For him, that clustering together had validity once. But today in the age of the automobile, with its advantages of mobility, communication, speed, the overcrowded city seemed outdated. "When we get into the city there we have to jam because the crowd is being herded and the herds are being pushed more and more together until the trampling of the herd is now the carbon dust rising from the herd as the carbon monoxide from the car. . . . So we want to do something about it. I did something about it when we went into the Broadacre City."

Broadacre was in reality no city at all, but a plan for dispersing civic, agrarian, industrial, cultural, educational, professional, and residential buildings throughout the landscape, widely spread, blending with forests, prairies, streams, whenever and wherever they might occur. Lasting results of the Broadacre project on the American scene include the streamlined service station, the off-highway motel, and the automobile-inspired suburban shopping center.

Frank Lloyd Wright's work, and the honors it brought, took him around the world, and he moved with ease everywhere. His genius was his passport, but it was an American passport first and last. Upon meeting the King of Iraq, and hearing the announcement: "His Royal Majesty, the King of Iraq." Frank Lloyd Wright stepped forward, bowed and extended his hand saying, "And here is His Majesty, the American Citizen."

His reaction to our British cousins was typically American in its blend of affectionate respect for their past and polite scorn for their vestigial present. His view of the French as substituting delicacy for soul articulates the muffled feelings of countless American tourists. Of Notre Dame in Paris he remarked in 1956, "It looks somehow smaller than I remembered." Toward the two cultures that impressed him most, Italian and Japanese, he was as frank and open in his admiration as a first-time tourist. "Italy is still the beating heart of the world of fine art." He wrote.

His mutual love affair with the Japanese reached an apex with the completion of the Imperial Hotel. He described his departure afterward as follows: "The dock at Yokohama, eighteen miles away, was reached by train [where I found that] sixty of the foremen had paid their own way down from Tokyo to shout again and wave good-bye, while they faded from sight as the ship went down the bay. Such people! Where else in all the world would such touching warmth of kindness be possible?"

Frank Lloyd Wright, American architect born in the Midwestern prairie and raised among its grasses, woodlands, and forests, could travel anywhere across the face of this earth and find, perceive and take great joy in the creative act wherever it occurred. Without any hindrance or preconception whatsoever, he could instantly feel a kinship and bond to the creative spirit anywhere. He erased time, limitation, and all barriers in the love and faith he had for the good, the true, and the beautiful.

MY COUNTRY RIGHT AND WRONG

Our Lack of Culture

We have nothing that we can point to today as an American culture, as a culture of our own which is the fruit of our own experience, of our own way of thinking and doing. Except these little things we call these buildings that we are building. I think it is quite a natural thing that it should have to take the form of buildings rather than any other form, say painting, or music even, or sculpture. Because building is next to our very flesh and bones. It is really nearer to man than any of the other great arts.

The difficulty comes when we get this thing started and get it going and get it visible to the elect—to those few who can see it. Then commercialization steps in, and it becomes an opportunity for exploitation, and the real essence of the thing has to be adulterated and passed around and made fit for general consumption. We have ruined more, wasted more, trampled on more than any civilization the world has ever seen—in a shorter time, too. An out of that trampling and out of the wreck, a little something will survive and grow by way of the experience such as you boys have here and are enjoying.

The poor Russians are not much better off than we were when we started. We began badly. Culture was not in our minds. We didn't have religion on our minds. We didn't have anything on our minds except to go out and bring in the bacon and make what is called a success. And it was easy, anybody could do it. When you look back at the lives of our big tycoons and these great so-called pioneers, what did they have? What was it that they had? Did they have spiritual insight? Did they have an experience of nature which revealed to them the integrities and beauties of nature? Not one. They had a persistent, go-getter, stand-patter, take-it, take-it, take-it, and they took it. That has resulted in great riches and great power—raw power, raw riches, everything raw.

Refinement isn't a word I like. Refinement is a suspicious circumstance that has been practised. There is something in the process of refining that destroys the essence of what is refined and throws the baby out with the bath water. So you have to be a little suspicious of refining this thing. But if these big fellows, big shots, if they had had this qualifying circumstance, what a culture this nation might have today!

There was one of them that had it, one of the great fellows who really had something of it and perhaps a good deal of it, and that was Marshall Field. Marshall Field was the only great force money power in the nation who had faith in the beautiful. He really introduced beauty into the mercantile world, and made it pay. And he became twice as rich, twice as influential and powerful as any of the other fellows because he had what in those days was referred to as taste. Marshall Field had taste. None of the other great merchants had it.

If we can turn that craze for quantity into a craze for quality, and make quality the *ne plus ultra* of the *E pluribus unum,* we will be doing a lot. And it doesn't take so many, when you look back and see the influence of Marshall Field as a merchant on the whole life of the period in which he lived. It was tremendous. Today I don't suppose we have any Marshall Fields to exercise that influence. Something seems to have come over the whole American scene that prostitutes it to the level of a commercial enterprise.

What is lacking now is this sense of quality as against quantity. We are swamped with quantity. And as I have often said and feel more bitterly as years go by, an original is only good in our country because out of it you can get any number of substitutes. We are known the world over as the nation of the substitute. I learned that when I was abroad this time— the nation of the substitute. Now why? Because there are so many of us? Because the rush is so great when it is on? For what we call success, and maybe power? I don't know what it is. I don't think you boys know, either. You haven't thought about it enough. But it is a very important thing that now we should know—what the hell it is that is eating us all up!

Why are we not as we imagine ourselves to be—the choice inspirer of the world along new lines of thought and feeling. Why in this very matter about which we are talking are South America, Mexico, and South American nations, Ireland, Finland, Switzerland all ahead of us. There is something deadly in this whole atmosphere in which we live now that we have got to tackle. I don't know that tackle is the right word—we have got to understand it, we have got to orientate ourselves in our work so that we don't fall into it.

(October 29, 1950)

America and Greece and Rome

This matter of publishing your work—see what it has done. See what I have done by doing it. Suppose I had never published anything, and they had to go and see the work itself. Wouldn't it have been a lot better, don't you think? If they couldn't see it photographed, and the only sight they could get of it was to go and see it actually, I think this movement would be very much further along. I think I owe an apology, even now, for the publication of my work. It enabled them to take it right out of the pages of the magazine without understanding at all what the thing means. Without understanding what is behind it, without getting hold of the basic principles that really made it.

It is a great thing to be able to hold your fire. To wait. Not join the scrimmage and the scramble. The best thing I know in the way of a perversion of English is that toot-and-scramble instead of that *toute ensemble*. Toot-and-scramble is what is ruining architecture and our country today. Nobody will wait. We have to have it now. They get married at the age of twenty-one or twenty-two or twenty-three and they soon have a couple of children and they have to go out and bring in the bacon and the pressure is increasingly great. Children have to have clothes—he has to earn money. Where is architecture in all that—behind the lighthouse. And what is the lighthouse? Money to live on, money for clothes, money for this, money for that.

Under the pressures of our economic system, all of the arts are a mere exploitation. I don't think today the creative artist is any more a feature of our civilization. We have got to bring it back. We have got to have at least a few fellows that are capable of demonstrating the value of creative art to our American people. I think we are way behind the European nations in that respect. Because everything is so easy, our country has a substitute for fine art. What would you say the substitute for fine art was in our country? I think what you see in the magazines, newspapers, radio, moving pictures, Hollywood. You can press a button and get yourself superficially entertained at any moment anywhere—washing dishes, going down the street, sitting in the hotel lobby, at the railroad station, on the train. Everything is on tap, flowing freely. And the real thing? I don't know if there is any use talking about the real thing when people are so lightly and easily satisfied. Where there is no real demand for the deeper thing and the finer thing, why not let them have less.

What is going to happen because of that shallow satisfaction? We are going to have a "style" again, a fashionable thing that everybody takes because everybody else has it. Nobody really understands it, but it becomes more and more respectable when the more influential people subscribe to it and have it. It is safe for those who have no feeling about it except to get in line. That is where our style is now. You have seen it, haven't you, what they call "modern." It is a curious manifestation or miscarriage of a great idea. It almost makes me sick of my own work, too, when I see so much of it everywhere misinterpreted. I think Phoenix is as good an example as you'll see in the world right here. Go down Central Avenue and see what you see. Go into the residence districts that are new and see what you see. On the way from here to town what you see is not very encouraging. Well, now, publication I think is responsible for a good deal of that.

I never like to think back to Rome, because Rome was already degenerate. But I think Rome in its day was where we are in our day, in relation to all the other great nations of the time. In Greece I am sure there must have been a different sense of things. And yet where is Greece today? What happened? Something happened. Has that question ever been satisfactorily answered, why Greece perished so soon? It was, next to ours probably, the shortest-lived civilization in history. Somehow we have lost roots. We don't have roots, we have recollections in place of roots. We have nostalgia and a kind of sentimentality in place of an urge for the real thing. Maybe it's all right, maybe it's a nice way to die without too much pain, gradually taper off into innocuous desuetude.

(December 17, 1950)

Education in America

If you are going to regard education as a tool of civilization to produce more civilization, I'll grant you that. But what is a civilization without a sense of beauty? What is a civilization content to be ugly? It lacks spirit, doesn't it. It is only an animal manifestation of man as an animal. Materialism, of course, ordered and made liveable. But when you name a university, you are pretending something else. Because God knows that universality, the sense of the universe and all that enters into it, is what a university should stand for. But our universities are nothing of that sort. They are no higher than any trade school in the nation.

[Robert Maynard] Hutchins tried to create one, didn't he, by way of the great books—ten great books that you would read and you were to absorb the wisdom of the ages from reading these books. And you were then supposed to be cultured. That was the supposition that he brought in. He was the young *enfant terrible* of education, you remember. He got in at the age of twenty-nine as President of the University of Chicago. And he hurled this idea into the ring. Well that got them all upset to think that a young fellow could come out and really make the whole system look like thirty cents and silly, by trying to improve upon it. I hope Hutchins doesn't ever hear this because he and I are friends.

But the fact remains that unless philosophy and art—and of course religion is the product of those two—unless those three things are predominant as experiences in the university, it isn't going to succeed in doing anything for beauty. It can do sanitation, it can do buildings, it can do all the machinery we need to do anything with, it can do something to regulate the relationships of man to man, physically, it can enact certain laws and of course set up a police force and set up a government. But who would want to live in it? I would rather go back to barbarism. Upon my soul I believe that barbarism is much handsomer and much more fun to live in than the kind of civilization without any of the other thing in it.

Could you imagine anything more dreary than modern civilization without anything of beauty in it at all? Just what they call practical. I can't think of anything more dead, more stupid, more of a thing I'd like to get away from. When I think of it I think of poles and wires along the street. I think of the roads they build and the way they build them. I think of the machinery they have to get around in. I think of the cars they design.

They try. I would be wrong if I said that they didn't try to make the things what we call good looking. And of course the ladies all want good looks. We have beauty parlors, don't we. And we have couturiers, dressmakers, and I guess everybody would admit that women's clothes today are a great improvement on anything they have ever been. Something has been done along that line a little. And of course we think in our buildings we have made progress. And all that belongs to this idea of culture, of course. Perhaps the beauty parlor is the only evidence of culture, along with the barber shop, that we have. What can you think of else?

Apprentice: Music?

Modern music? Well we aren't producing any of it to speak of—not enough to talk about. It is like our architecture. You grant us a beginning in architecture, and I'll grant you a beginning in music. But you see music and architecture are not on the same footing at all where culture is concerned. Architecture is basic to culture. Music is an attribute of culture; so is painting, so would sculpture be. But architecture you experience, the other things you accede to.

Without architecture you can't have a culture. And of course it is only lately that this has become manifest. It is only the ideal we hold of an organic architecture that can sustain and justify all these assumptions. Because when architecture is on a plane where it comes from within outward, there you have the basis of a culture. As architecture has been, I wouldn't call it the basis of a culture because it has all been parasitic and derivative. It has been an eclecticism and not therefore basic in any sense—a mere case of fashion and a feeling for the moment, a thing on the perimeter instead of something coming out from a soul that is of man.

So with this new sense of architecture as organic comes a responsibility deeper, more profound, than ever existed in the life of an architect before, because we have now taken him out of the parasitic realm and we are heading him into the world of creation. We are making of him a creative individual. And I assume he must be so, because only the creative individual can produce from within outward this way.

Don't you see that all the architecture of Sir Christopher Wren, Michelangelo—well Mike invented a little bit, he was imaginative—but almost all of that was finding something here or there, picking it up and putting it on something. Nothing was born, in other words. Nothing new came out to make life better, worth living, and more lovely in itself. Wasn't it all the old box, decorated?

The only thought of architecture until organic architecture came alive was just a box, wasn't it. Isn't Le Corbusier's work and thought today just a box? What else is it? Get the box up on stilts. Did that justify it? Does it make it any better looking to put legs under it, skinny legs? I don't think it does. But you see the thought isn't changed. The thought is the same. It is only in organic architecture that the thought really has changed. It has substantially and practically and absolutely rejected the box as symbolic or necessary in architecture. Now once that step is taken, you are in a new world entirely. You are in a world that democracy has made possible.

But where is democracy? Where is it in the state of Wisconsin now for instance? What has happened to it all over the United States? Just as we get into an architecture worthy of democracy, democracy goes to pot. So there is a fix.

Apprentice: Mr. Wright, wasn't Thomas Jefferson going to take care of all that through education?

Yes, and my people all worship the idea of education. Education was going to cure all the evils of the world. And Thomas Jefferson built a university, but he did not specify what he himself was thinking that was truly cultural. And I think Thomas Jefferson had an idea that education was necessarily a culture. He didn't foresee these universities as we have set them up and practised them now. Thomas Jefferson would be horrified to see that public comfort station they erected to his memory. I don't think he would feel that the thing was a realization of his dreams. I think he would look upon that Greek memorial to Lincoln without very much pleasure either. In fact I think he would look at the state capital with some degree of horror. He was quite choosy in his day, if you could read what he said about the buildings at Williamsburg. The most drastic criticism you ever read. He ridiculed them from bottom to top. And then he build Monticello.

Well now to me it is because education has not been a culture that we are in a fix. I think that is what is the matter. Because how can you send—let's take Wisconsin—how can you send fifteen or twenty thousand provincials, graduates of little schools around this state and then figure out a system by which they can be divided into classes of some several hundred in a class up to a thousand and sit them there together and really do anything for them in the way of development? By just letting them sit in a classroom, take part in a curriculum, and be indoctrinated by something that is considered good medicine for the mob? Because isn't that all they can do? What more can they do? A few fellows whose curiosity is aroused can gather around one of the professors and ply him with a few questions and have them answered. They would be the ones that got something out of it.

Now what else is it? Of course it is the best marriage mart we have. It's the basis where boy meets girl now better than anywhere else. And most of the girls go to college for that purpose, I think. I think a few of them go there for what they call an education, but I think most of them go there to meet the boys. And I think the dessicated principles which are dealt out to that fifteen thousand or twenty thousand students by rule of thumb, by rote, what are they?

How many of you have been to universities? Well, pretty nearly everybody. I was there myself, but I quit. Three months—if I had stayed I would have had a degree as an engineer. I couldn't wait. I wanted to be an architect, and I give you my word to this day I can't do a simple problem in algebra to save my life from perdition. And I don't think it is necessary. I don't think I missed anything.

I said when they wanted to define an engineer that an engineer was just a rudimentary, undeveloped architect. And that I believe. The engineer comes in with the letters, and with a dot to put on the i maybe, although probably not. But the architect writes the words, and what are the engineer's letters worth without those words?

(October 15, 1952)

DEMOCRACY IN AMERICA

Democracy and Aristocracy

I've been reading Walt Whitman this morning. I didn't know he was a critic, but he criticized everything, lengthwise, crosswise, and very intelligently in very turgid English, as bad as mine I assure you. I think any modern writer reading Whitman's English—the English he used in criticizing—would say he was a worse writer than I.

He was taking Shakespeare apart this morning for me and I was wishing Charles Laughton was here—he might take up the cudgels for Shakespeare. And he declared that Shakespeare was the prophet, the, what shall I say, not apotheosis in himself, but he was the poet of aristocracy. He was the poet of the king, the prince, the beautiful building, all that which humanity in European days, Medieval days I guess, or probably just subsequent to Medieval days, had achieved. He was the poet of the aristocrat. And all his commoners, while wonderfully drawn, and all his jewelry and all his wonderful weaving was illustrative of that condition which existed during his lifetime. So he was the poet of the duke, the prince, the grand seigniors, and his land was all laid out formally, the gardens with walks, and I think the concluding line was "and plenty of Japonicas." And you walked amid wonderful masses of flowers in bloom, and trees trimmed, grass cut, everything civilized to a point that the grand seignior would have it.

And when he kicked in all the lowly characters which he did so deftly, I think you won't find them painted any more clearly anywhere else in all of literature. He always made them amusing to the upper classes and the concomitant of aristocracy. And I never thought of it before, myself, but it is true. You seldom see Shakespeare celebrating the simple and the common and the process of becoming. There's nothing in Shakespeare that would prophesy democracy. The idea of a democracy could never have originated with a mind like Shakespeare's. But he was the greatest painter, the greatest and most deft characterizer probably who ever lived, and the greatest artist, therefore. But to the greatest artist who ever lived, democracy would never have occurred. Well, what does that mean? That's rather sinister.

Maybe we are all headed back toward aristocracy again. And I just caught myself up too because when they asked me for a definition of democracy I replied that it was the highest form of aristocracy the world has ever seen. Why? Because it is aristocracy innate with the individual, of the individual, and maintained by him every hour of his life. And he cannot pass it on, it is no privilege conferred upon him. It is really him, or it doesn't exist.

There you have Shakespeare's primitive aristocracy developing into a completed, final and absolute aristocracy. So maybe Whitman was dead right. And in the little footnote which I read appended to the criticism I was reading—"Some Thoughts on Shakespeare" he calls it—there is a statement that the idea of democracy is to get the great individual from the masses, so condition the masses and so administer the laws that the great individual naturally proceeds from the masses to this estate. What do you call that? What would you call that type of law, that kind of government that would best promote and establish that kind of thing? You'd have to place a premium, wouldn't you, on individuality. You would have to establish your institutions in such a manner that wherever it existed, it would be encouraged to come out.

Woman Guest: Isn't that what you have proved in yourself, Mr. Wright?

What's that?

Woman Guest: That's what you have proved. You have reached the aristocracy stage now.

My dear Lady, I don't know what I've proved. I think nothing as yet. I consider myself the champion failure of our era, and proud of it.

I think we are making a mistake now. I think we have gone off the beam. I do not believe that we are democratic anymore. I think we have lost the original vision of our forefathers, and I think when we centralize, federalize, we lose the very thing we are born to maintain. And I think we cannot, in a democracy, hero worship very much. I think we have to be careful of heroes. And I don't think we should ever do what we do with a President today, make him a hero and worship him as a giver of form, when all he was ever intended to be by the forefathers was an executive.

All the tendency today that you see everywhere is toward Shakespeare's form of aristocracy, not the democratic aristocracy that I have been talking about so. It isn't talked of, it isn't written about, the press is silent concerning it, you hear nothing of it anywhere. You don't see much of it either. It is pretty well under cover. But I feel that if there is anything in this idea of democracy, we don't understand it. We've given it very little attention, and no analysis outside of men like Whitman, men like Emerson, men like Melville. I think the great preachers in the early days had it, most of them, especially the Unitarians—I think they had it. I don't know who else has it now. The churches of course are out. Religion has folded up and been neatly put away by science.

When we got the machine and when we got science going as we have it going so that the very streets crawl with it even out into the tenth mile beyond the center of the city, and when gadgetry is everywhere, the oven, the washing machine, the ice box, not to mention the deep freeze, what have we? There we have gone, and there is where we live. And we have not taken pains to keep up with it ourselves. There is nothing in us that is congruous with the machine except our lack of imagination, perhaps, and initiative.

The machine has no initiative. The machine can feel or imagine nothing. And of course the tendency of an employer of the machine as a tool is to become more and more like the tool he uses. So in this apparently innocent and harmless looking thing you have in your hand and call a tool, when it develops to the point where it becomes a robot, look out. And the time has come for us to look out.

We are not looking out. We are becoming more and more hybridized. We are becoming more and more unable to do this thing, to accomplish this thing called democracy. What is that old slang phrase, "hoist by his own petard"? Well that is something like what is happening to us in our civilization today. We are really being butchered by the very thing that we would use to butcher by, and we are not aware of it, and we don't seem to care. It is that latter that distresses me as an artist, as an architect. And I think that is why the artist today is more or less a shenanigan, an evasion, a skate of some kind, cheap or expensive. And why all this thing that we were founded to cherish—and we were too at the time—was very much alive, and it was operative. And the individual was likely to come forth, because the conditions were such that he might. But less and less is that opportunity open, and more and more are you all conditioned to the herd level. Out of the present course we are pursuing by way of these great advantages of ours, this great advantageous tool we call the machine, is now coming, inevitably, fascism or communism.

Democracy was a dream, a beautiful dream which was enjoyed, and they made sacrifices to it too, in their day. They lived for it, they believed in it, and they had faith that it would come. This is something new in human life, this idea of the great success of the manipulator, the great success of the herdsman. It's the herdsman now that drives the herd, and out of the herdsman who has had very little to qualify him as a driver of the herd, we are going to get whatever culture we can find.

(April 12, 1953)

The Common Man

I never have met a man who said he was a common man unless he was uncommon. You see the point?

Woman Guest: It's very difficult.

Well, that's my difficulty. And people write in and want me to give them an article for nothing in rebuttal and I will not. But I am willing to talk in the morning at the Fellowship on any subject that occurs to me, and this morning it's the common man again. I'd like to get it straight with the Fellowship, anyhow. Now there is no fellowship in the common man, I mean, there is no common man in the Fellowship! That's apparent. And as for a common woman, Oh God!

So it occurred to me, as I sat down here, that these flowers they are of common nature but uncommon in the sense that I am speaking of the uncommon man. The grass is the common man. The primitive, elemental, simple, good material for civilization. And, of course, he is abundant, of course he is everywhere. Of course there could be no democracy without him, and democracy was invented for him. We are a democracy because of our—now I've to be careful about the word—feeling for the common man. That man in general, in generate, you might say, like the grass on the ground, like the elemental growth of nature, is there in nature to be cultivated in civilization. To be developed into the ideal thing which is the possession of, not the common man but the uncommon man.

Now that's a good story. If you'll take that over, I think that will hold water. I believe that's what democracy, felt and said too, concerning what we call the common man. Of course you know that famous quarrel between—it was a debate between—Thomas Jefferson and Alexander Hamilton. Alexander Hamilton was the old aristocrat that regarded the common man as simply there to feather their nest and make life a little easier for them. That was the old aristocratic idea.

But the democratic aristocratic idea was that the true aristocrat would be a man embracing in him the future—the character, even the fate of the common man. And that his governors, his interpreters, his instructors, his education would consist in proceeding from the common man to the uncommon man. And that the aristocracy of democracy would consist of the uncommon man developed from the common man.

Well, Alexander Hamilton declared that what would happen has happened. He foresaw it and I think Thomas Jefferson agreed with him. But Thomas Jefferson thought he had the remedy: education. Said Hamilton, "You must qualify the vote. You cannot let by and sundry and everybody vote, whether they are qualified to vote, whether they understand what they are voting for or whether they do not—you will soon have mediocrity rising into high places."—a way of quantity, rather than quality. Well, he was right, of course, and then Thomas Jefferson's rebuttal was, yes, he admitted that, but we will protect the vote by our educational system, by what we call education.

Well, of course, we know now it hasn't done it. We have not been protected by education. But who would be so bold as to declare that education was planned on the basis of Thomas Jefferson's idea of what it ought to be. I think just the reverse is true. It has become more or less that. A university is a trade school. You go there to get prepared for a job of some kind. You don't get acquainted with yourself as a human being, you are not tutored in what you are and what you may become, nor are you very well acquainted with principles, and as far as culture is concerned your education is not on speaking terms with culture.

Never have I thought of an educated man as a cultured man, a cultured human being. Well now, Thomas Jefferson regarded him as such. That was our American aristocrat: the man cultured by this ideal of freedom and by the growth of his own conscience to become not a yes man, not a committee meeting mind, but a single man, as Emerson described him. A single man. A man who could stay put on an idea that he had of his own and believe in it and work with it and for it. In other words, the man who could be alone and who could subscribe to an idea.

So it occurs to me that the best way to describe the uncommon man, in the sense that I am using the term, is the man who can fall in love with an idea, the man who can subscribe to an idea and who realizes the nature of an idea. Now there is your uncommon man as I refer to him. Now you can find him driving a truck. You can find him like our George, the stone mason. You can find him anywhere, as I've found him all my life in architecture, on the job and frequently in the early days he used to call me Frank. And I liked it.

Now out of this and out of that liberal condition will grow the American aristocrat, because the world cannot live without aristocracy. The world cannot live without distinctions, superiorities and inferiorities. They are bound to occur because they are planted there in nature. All nature seems to be a race for the superior, for the excellent, for the finer specimen of the thing whatever it may be. And we cannot escape it in civilization.

Of course civilization is an abstraction, isn't it? We're taking nature as one of these flowers would be taken and making a pattern of what we consider to be characteristic and beautiful in the flower. Now that's what we're trying to do with civilization, and education is the instrument we are using to that end, and it doesn't know it. I have never heard it mentioned. I've never heard it brought forth unless by Emerson or Walt

Whitman or somebody like that. Certainly not in the educational region or realm. We are trying to produce—we don't know what exactly—by a means which we have learned by rote, not by experience. We've learned what we have learned mostly from books, from the experience of other peoples in other times and under other conditions than democratic ones. Democracy has always been floating on the top of society, but always by the way of men like Rousseau and John Paul Richter: the poets, the philosophers, the artists. That is where it has come down to us. What we have cherished today are the beautiful buildings we have built, the beautiful thoughts that we have . . . you wouldn't say "thunk," would you—but thought, and so on.

Is it the emanations of the common man that fill our libraries and our art galleries and our studios, universities? No. It is a sort of cream, I imagine, that rises by way, through this element of the common to the level of the uncommon, and becomes the treasured possession of the race. And it's always going to be so, because it's nature, because it's our nature, and we cannot escape it.

(August 24, 1958)

Democracy and Politics

At last I believe we're going to have a chance to vote for a superior man in the White House. I don't know how many of you heard that acceptance speech of Adlai Stevenson's in which he bravely stood there and declared that what we needed now is a new America. Now no mere politician would ever have said a thing like that. It's what I myself believe because the old America that we had is being entirely captured by mediocrity in high places. I believe that would be true even of the presidency today, and I think a little brains, a mind such as Adlai Stevenson possesses [might save us]. I don't think he's a winner, I don't think he's popular. I doubt if he ever pleases the common man because he doesn't belong with the common man, except as the common man is the foundation of progress.

How long ago have we had a real mind in the White House? We can't say despite all Eisenhower's good points that he has a fine mind, a great mind—he hasn't. And his whole background is military, and for the State Department I can't imagine anything more detestable. Adlai Stevenson's background is more than excellent; he's been a splendid governor of Illinois, courageous in the same way that he was when he was making his acceptance speech. I felt I might have written a good deal of it myself, it was so coincident with what I myself feel is the matter with the country.

Of course we are wide open, we're vulnerable; democracy has its weak side. And its weak side is that no device has ever been put forward to prevent this thing that has happened to us—mediocrity in high places. And if mediocrity succeeds in ruling the United States, we're going to be the lowest form of socialism the world has ever seen—lower than communism. And what protection have we, because politics is numerical. Politics depends on your getting the most votes in the next election. And how are you going to get the most votes at the next election? What is the only recipe for getting the most votes? To reach the most people. And to reach the most people we can't say that most people are superior, can we? We could say that superiority means a product of numbers, but numbers and quality are never on speaking terms. They don't belong together.

So either we go up in the direction of a finer and higher quality of manhood and statesmanship or else we go down, down, down, lower and lower to the average, even below the average. Because unfortunately the average would rather go down than go up, and if you do not believe that statement, why just look about and see what happens by the law of gravitation. Being architects you should be on at least speaking terms with the law of gravitation. Now politics is subject to deterioration, is subject to the law of gravitation. It requires continuous courageous renewal and appeal to the spirit in order to keep the thing high and keep it growing.

So if we're going to keep our country growing, we must have a mind in the White House. We haven't a mind there now who would know a good building from a bad building. When it came up what was to be done with the atom investigation and all our expenditures of billions of dollars on the research concerning the atom, he was for turning it over to the established order by way of these service companies of the United States, which have always stood between the people and their rights. In other words the pole and wire men were to have the atom bomb. The research system to be turned over to them. That doesn't look to me like a very good brain, it looks to me altogether too Republican. The Republicans have always represented the financial interests and the financial security "so-called" of the American people.

Anyway it's not within my province to criticize beyond my depth, but I'm sure that unless we do have this superior mind and the superior thing and maintain it against all odds, no matter how heavy they are, we're not going to last very long as a democracy.

(August 19, 1956)

CITIES IN AMERICA

The Modern American City

Maybe the modern city is one of the symptoms of what's the matter with us. It is really just the antique city, isn't it, with just gadgetry inside and out. What else is it? What one single modern thing have we, the American people, free, with a new great gift of ground, unspoiled—the Indians did not spoil it. We were fortunate; they were nomads. We didn't have any wreckage to clear away. We got the whole country. We brought over the Medieval city and planted it as the English had conceived it in the dormitory towns. What we got to start with was the English dormitory town. Now what have we done with it? We have crammed it with automobiles, poles and wires, gadgetry of all sorts, and the old city is still right there. There has been no change in it.

That is why we modeled Broadacre City in 1932. We were trying to do something about it, we were trying to see along the line of this inevitable change that is taking place, that is taking place right now in the lives of every one of you. Everything about you is in a process of becoming, as Heraclitus said. But we have done nothing about it in regard to our cities, to our civilizations, to our way of life. The old thing is still there, and while it did its work beautifully in the Middle Ages, it was a Medieval cultural agent. Would you say that the city today is a modern cultural agent? Would you say it was necessary to our culture as a free people? Would you? If so, in what respect? It is now, isn't it, a demoralization. Isn't it an interference and an exaggeration of the herd instinct? Isn't it there purely because of animal hangover? Not because of any virtue which it has for us today.

What makes this habitual to and fro, coming and going, always coming, always going, living on the outskirts, driving in, driving back? Wouldn't you think that by this time, with all the media of intercommunications, and all this facility of travel, and everything we have been given by science, that wouldn't be necessary any longer? It seems to me almost ridiculous. But the architects are not doing anything about it. Have you heard anything from the architects either near or far concerning the situation? Have they applied their thinking apparatus to it, in any sense? Yes, Corbu did, he piled it up higher and higher and thought it was all right to just take the Medieval city and carry it just as high as it would stand, never thinking of the consequences at the base of the exaggeration. He created a condition that might be expected of a good old institution gone to hell. Which is practically what it has done.

We go to New York and see these great towers standing up there all over the place, like fingers threatening the sky. What do they mean? Have you ever thought what these tall things standing there mean, so thickly crowding one another, bursting up out of the soil, a crude manifestation of something never planned? Their relationship was never thought of. Every man for himself and the devil for the hindmost. The fellow that could get there first and get the tallest was lead one in this game of concentrated ownership. What good has it done him?

If you want to build tall, and there is no reason why you shouldn't build tall—to build tall is beautiful—the buildings should be reasonably situated and beautiful in themselves. The city skyscrapers aren't. They all crowd one another. All you see is the top. And they are creating a condition below that is deadly. After the atom bomb came into the tool box, along with the other tools that we haven't learned to use, then what? That concentration is plain murder, isn't it. Because some fool someday is going to do what Harry Truman did with Hiroshima. Some mediocre mind in high places is going to drop that bomb. And that will be the wreck of all the concentrations now existing. They can't carry it too far, as there will be plenty of people left living, I guess, and in out of the way places. But I doubt that when the bomb breaks out, there is single city left in Europe or America. Africa may escape. So if we don't have more wisdom than is manifest in these manifestations of power, [we are in trouble]. In New York City, these great tall buildings are increasing in height and increasing in number. They are now taking down the Central Station and, where hundreds of people are now, putting in thousands right in the heart of the city, accenting a centralization that is inevitable in the line of natural destruction or else by violent death. And yet it goes on. Nothing can stop it.

If we had architects in the place where they should be we would have had a solution of all this, not centuries ago, but certainly fifty years ago. Maybe a hundred years ago was the time. Well it isn't too late yet, because these are only little hot spots dotted over a great expanse of the most beautiful territory perhaps in the world. If there is any most beautiful territory, we have it. And we have done nothing with it. And there it is a problem now, an interesting one to tackle. But who is calling for a solution? Anybody? They are quite satisfied, quite proud. I think that they quite enjoy the pandemonium and the commotion.

You can see these prairies now becoming misty, musty, a threat to human nature. Of course some day they are going to throttle that engine—

now instead of hoofs we have the combustion engine. If they do humanize the engine and save us from the poisons that it generates, that is not a solution of the problem, is it. The problem is really extremely serious. The traffic problem can never be solved, because the traffic problem is our modern gadgetry infringing on the antique city, isn't it. Now the width of the streets, the placing of the buildings, the centralizing of everything to a common point, all that was utterly habitual and unthinking. It foresaw nothing that has transpired, did it.

I don't believe there was a single idea or a single thought parallel to the law of change working from the time we discovered this country up to the present moment. If so, let's see, if we can find something, something that we have really contributed according to this inevitable law of change taking place even at the time we discovered the country. I have tried but I cannot think of anything.

We have all sorts of new ways of doing old things. Lots of old ways of doing new things. But what have we really created in the way of civilization? It's a totally inconsistent thing, totally contrary to everything that you could name as scientific. Science, of course, is supposed to be sensible, isn't it. Art might be foolish and religion may be mystic, but science is always sensible, I believe. Supposed to be, isn't it. Well now science has taken this whole thing apart and it is characteristic of science that it can take anything apart but it never can put anything together again so it will live. If you want it to live, you have to call upon the creative artist, or the prophet, the preacher, the seer. He seems to be there where life is for the purpose of making more of it, and making something out of it too. But the scientist is not. The scientist is there just to see how it is made, take it apart and see how many things you can get out of it. Somebody else has to come and say what to do with it after they get through strewing the parts around. Something like taking a car into a garage and the mechanic there will take it all apart and spread it all over the floor of the garage and wouldn't know how to put it together again. That is the position we are in right now.

(March 13, 1955)

New York City

The enormity of New York City connected with New Jersey, when you take the two together, is enormity added to enormity in every sense of the word. I imagine that Sodom and Gomorrah would be an elegy in a country churchyard compared with New York City. In its present state it is just a great wrangle of everything you can imagine. One thing impinging on another—stop and go. You go out just in order to come back, and you come back just in order to go out. Garbage cans are on the sidewalk waiting to be collected. Every taxicab blind to the style of the private car. An utterly senseless exaggeration of what we call our advantages, to the point where we are going to die of them, inevitably, unless you boys get busy when you get a little older and do something about it. The trouble is there are no architects—they do not have any. The architects today are merchants, everything is merchantable. Everybody is selling either himself or something else. Very little ideology. Very little above the belt can be found anywhere in New York City.

Of course, there must be enough there to hold it together, because it is hanging together for a while. But when you see what the engineer did to it in the first place, when you see that great jangle of trusses overhead, freeways, highways, bridges badly designed, buildings looming everywhere—prison towers for the poor, the poor being built in permanently—it is not a very cheering spectacle. Everything is just about an hour from everything else. In spite of all the continuity, in spite of all the proximity, you have to go a long way to get anything, get anywhere. Not long enough!

(September 9, 1957)

Housing and the American Dilemma

Well, this is housing convention week. Let's have a housing convention here this morning. They're having a housing convention in Chicago, there's one in St. Louis and one in Tucson, housers from all over the United States. They seem a little bit worried about something. I don't know what it is. I'm sure it's not the design of the thing. I guess the profits are tailing. I myself have written a piece on housing to go in *Esquire* and I bet you a dollar it never gets there. Housing—the word has an evil sound, doesn't it. Housing. Something like stabling.

You know I've discovered more and more where the iniquity came upon us, where we fell into it. You know London has what they call a "dormitory town" and in the London dormitory town is everything you see in our country in what we call housing and the way we build our houses: lot beside lot, house with its toes practically on the sidewalk. We added a front yard, we pushed it back a little way, that we did. All the rest is really London housing, just as nearly everything else is. The clothes we wear—where did we get those? Everything we have is English, but not very good English. They at least wear their clothes very nicely, carelessly and becomingly. We don't. But everything we've got we got somewhere. We've never done anything of our own for ourselves except to cram this English idiom in architecture with gadgetry. It's got all the gadgetry it can now hold, and there it is still in the old form.

The houser runs out, cuts the piece up into lots—the smaller the lots and bigger the profit can be to the houser—and there it is, when land all over the country is so unoccupied. These cities make little hot spots all over the country, and it seems that our population is gauged by those hot spots. We travel for hours through empty space and never think anything about it. But when we get into the city we have to jam because the crowd is being herded and the herds are being pushed more and more together until the trampling of the herd is now the carbon dust rising from the herd as the carbon monoxide from the car. We have recently come from Philadelphia, which is the worst instance, I guess, of the crowding of the herd in the whole world. I think you could put Philadelphia up against London. They are the two prime examples, and one came from the other. Philadelphia is a little imitation London.

We want to do something about it. I did something about it when we went into Broadacre City. We tried to head off the herd, tried to prevent the stampede, and we are still doing it. In Chicago there is another contribution, the prefab. Prefabrication has taken everybody's interest now in the housing industry, and the conventions are all primarily concerned with the prefabricated house. Now, of course, the prefabricated house is inevitable, and a good thing. You've got the machine, or rather, the machine has got us where it wants us, pretty nearly. It got us serving the great crowd en masse, mass designs, pack them away, pack 'em in. All freedom is gone. There is nothing in the whole system now that is really American. If America is for the free man, then he doesn't have a home. So what are we going to do about it ourselves?

When you chaps get out the first thing you want to have in your mitt is the desire for space. Without space how can you bring up decent, healthy children? How can you have a happy family? How can you build a house that is worth looking at without space? You can't. If you want good design, the basis for it is spaciousness. And it's got to look spacious and be spacious and be a part of where it stands. Well, look at it. See Levittown. See any of these attempts they are making to pack people away in proximity to cities—even in suburbs. Or if they go out where there is a factory and the factory has housing, it's all on the same pattern. They seem to know nothing except to put them side by side as close as you can get them. You can hear from one to the other, you can see from one to the other, and then they put a big picture window in the front of each house right across the street so you can see right down the length of the whole interior. And they have no feeling whatever for what we would call space.

Well, space being the essence of good architecture, we've got to have a change in all this, because I don't believe it's good enough for America. I think there are a lot of things that require reconsideration—that's probably the first one. We can go after our clothes afterward—they need reconsideration, too. I sympathize with that poor man who committed suicide. He said he was tired of all this buttoning and unbuttoning, and so it is. We're all tired of this buttoning and unbuttoning in housing, because that's what it amounts to.

So, what would be the plan? I remember—I don't know how many years ago (I can't count the years any more except by tens)—the year when I put into the field the quadruple block plan. I put the houses in groups of four, with their back yards close together, not too close, decently separated. I finally put them close together in the plan for Philadelphia or Pittsfield, I think it was, but even then they had an acre all around each house. That was in the *Ladies Home Journal*. We made it the basis for the Broadacre City layout, but nobody ever noticed it.

Where do these housers get their designs? How do they get that way? It is from the magazines they peruse, and the magazines publish the work of little boys in the back rooms, inferior architects. What would be the source of their supply? I've often wondered. Some of them don't have architects at all, do they? I notice the lumber yards will sell you plans for a house. They are stockpiled and become a cliche right way. But where does the original cliche come from? Did they add to it anything that has been done since the London dormitory town? I can't see anything, except the gadgetry, of course. And the gadgetry, like the automobile, makes the plan all the worse now—makes the condition of the householder almost unbearable.

Now that we have speed, we have a new scale, a new time scale instead of a new scale of feet and inches. Say ten miles in ten minutes; that would be pretty fast driving, or would it? Say ten miles in fifteen minutes or five miles in ten minutes. What does that mean? Everybody in the country is going to have one car at least—every man, woman and child in all probability over fourteen, so some families will have four or five. Some families now have three, don't they, two or three? Whereas we gauge the house by the number of cars—1-car house, 2-car house, 3-4-5-car house—5-car house is luxury. Now what would be super luxury? A 10-car house! So it goes. Now think about it a little bit and see where it's heading in, what's going to happen. Do you think young America is going to give up the motor car? Not on your life. Even mother wouldn't give it up for anything, not even a mink coat.

Wherever you've got it, it's going to stand and it's going to grow, and it is growing. Don't you see them coming in in fives, all piled up one on top of the other, anywhere you go, new ones coming in, the used car lots taking up most of the empty space in the cities now. Why is it, tell me, that no one speaks out about it? They all complain and mutter, and put up with it, and nothing is being done about it at all that I know. Have you read anything or seen anything in the architectural magazines solving the parking problem, except to clear off adjoining lots and let them pile the cars up and blot out the building? You can't build a building, a beautiful building, and put in it a whole acreage of cars. Then what have you got? Nothing.

I suppose the idea of the skyscraper is to get away from the car, and if you look at the building about fifty feet above the street maybe you can see it. So the skyscraper perhaps is the only escape from the car. And yet when that skyscraper is emptied and when you get to it every foot of height is an embarrassment because those people are all dumped into the car below and dumped out of the car into the building above. So that's been a very bad practise, unless there is space enough around it to accommodate the population of the building.

That's one of the things for you fellows to think about, isn't it. That's where you ought to begin now your adventure into the architecture of the future—the parking problem. What to do with the man and his car. In his car he's got to get around, you know, he has to move and he has to have space enough around him so he can. So wouldn't you say he'd bulk about one hundred times an area to what he used to bulk on his feet? How many times do you think would be fair? Think it over. And look at the car he has now, the length of it, look at the shape of it. That's where his heart is now.

The American car has become fantastic because of what the American doesn't know about life. And I am sorry to say that probably he doesn't care, either. He hasn't thought about it. You fellows have to do the thinking about it if you are architects. That, as I understand it, is what architects are for. They are to think out these problems and work out solutions that are practicable in the true sense of the word—not as a realtor would put it. What is practical to him is all a different thing from what really is practical to human beings. But you boys are all in service of the human being, and the human being of the future, not just of the present. We don't build houses for today, we don't build houses for ten years from now. The houses we like to build are good for 300 years and they ought to last as far forward as you can see for twenty-five years, anyway. Isn't that fair? If you are going to build a good house, and going to put your life into it and put the other lives into the life you put into the house, well, twenty-five years is a narrow margin. It's really a pressing, desperate problem.

Think about it, see what comes to your mind concerning it. See if you have any ideas concerning it. What's going to happen when the human being bulks now 100 to 1 in his necessity for establishment to what he did ten years ago? What's going to happen to his house, what's going to happen to his city, what's going to happen to his whole life? And I don't see anybody answering. Mies van der Rohe says there is nothing human about a building at all. Somebody asked him if he'd like to see those things he had designed built by the mile. He made a gesture, his favorite gesture, and said, "Yes, by the mile, by ten miles." He'd like to see it all standardized and humanity caged.

The answer isn't going to come from there. The answer isn't going to come from any architecture architect-perpetrated that I know anything about. Le Corbusier has been adding to the distress of every city in which he has built. He even takes it out into the Hindu desert and practises the same thing—he only knows one thing. So the American architect has to come up with something else, and that's what he's got to start with. We're quite sure that the idea is good and the suggestion is valid anyway—that you can make something beautiful out of the car and getting to places in it and getting to places away from it and have it independent and free as a thing of pleasure and enjoyment. But you've got to start with it and you can't do that in the city. If you get a start with it, a start with the problem, you can do something with it and we can solve it. But it has destroyed the city, and the city is just waking up to the fact that something is hurting, something is wrong.

Now, what's the city going to do? They are tearing down blocks in Chicago. The University has given Zeckendorff forty-five acres to develop—now he's a developer. Let's see what he does with it. He won't do anything, can't. They'll make decent looking buildings, but they won't solve the parking problem. If he did there wouldn't be very much doing on those forty-five acres. It would all either be a parking lot or a little green park, one of the two—preferably a green park. They should build nothing on it, and so with all the cities. Those little green parks and those little parking spaces would save the city for another ten years, maybe, but that is about all. Let's see you get these little green parks anywhere. The university could contribute this one, couldn't it, it could afford to, but now it's going to be built up just as tight or tighter than anything in the city. But built better—not a slum. They'll do the latest apartment buildings, probably ten, twelve, fifteen or twenty stories high, and then where is the parking? They can dig down in the ground, they can go three stories below and can burrow into the earth. They can do all these things. Suppose, say, that the building now starts on the second floor—that's the first story, and all the rest beneath that is parking. That wouldn't be enough, you wouldn't solve the problem. Well, suppose we say the city now should start at the fifth floor—that might serve for a little while, but it too wouldn't work.

I think architecture in our cities is now unthinkable. What's going to happen? We know now that we can go ten miles in ten minutes. We know where to go, but everywhere we start going, we the people, the realtor gets the idea into his system before we can get there. Out he goes, buys it all up, cuts it up into little lots, pushes up the price way up high so you are defeated right there and you become a suburb. So he is the champion—not the inventor—the profit maker where the suburb is concerned, and the suburb isn't the answer.

Apprentice: What is the solution?

The solution is Broadacre City. The solution is there is no city any more. We don't need it. It used to have a purpose in life when personal contact was essential to culture, when there was no other way of getting it. Now it is in the way of culture. Now you have television, telephone, motor car, airplane, life, the whole thing has been sort of volatilized, don't you see, where it used to be all dense and solid, and necessarily so, and the city was planned for that. That's what our modern cities were planned for originally, and we copied it, and that's where we made our deadly mistake. Now it's all a farce.

(February 16, 1958)

The New American Village

Leaving the city we lose nothing whatever except congestion, a lack of privacy, and frustration. By way of electrification, and now television, we will pretty soon not have to leave home to get the greatest benefit education can confer upon us, far more than the crowding could ever have given us in the past. No matter where we go now we are in touch with and can be the recipient of all these riches which accrue from, or used to accrue from, the big city.

While it takes a long time to modify human habit, that modification is taking place in spite of all our habituations. And if we look carefully we will see it working now. We will see that the best people are leaving the city and going the country way. We see that even the merchants are realizing that they cannot do business in a pile of hardware, like the cars. They have to move out and they are moving out. But they make a little repetition of cubicles, taking the worst of the city out into the country.

The little wayside gas station was perhaps the first visible evidence of decentralization. But now the decentralization everywhere is cumulative. It's increasing like an undertow. Now that has its gospel. These changes that occur so silently and tremendously throughout the life of humanity all have to be met with a new philosophy. We are without a philosophy now to meet these changes which are inevitable and occurring everywhere. And it is from architecture that the philosophy must come. We do not get it from statesmanship. We do not get it from our literary men. Our poets seem to be unaware of what is taking place. The architect must, by way of this station and his stature, be the man, be the one, the agent who now can, with a little prophecy and more work, awaken this nation to what it really is headed for.

Anything that increases the potency, the significance, the value of the individual home as a democratic unit will make it richer, more pleasant to live in. Beauty is a word we use reluctantly now for fear we will be dubbed sentimentalists. But beauty is the object of it all. To make the village life a beautiful life, a home in the village more characteristic of the freedom that we profess, greater privacy must go with freedom. Freedom is not a thing without conscience and freedom with conscience is what we are striving to establish. What does freedom with conscience mean? It means the life of each individual is inviolate as concerned with other individuals.

That right for all is Democracy. If we work out a philosophy of Democracy, and if we work it out along that line, we will find the reality missing in our social outlook today. Occasionally we will see it touched upon and occasionally we will see it being built: we will see these evidences of maintaining individuality in spite of the great drift toward standardization. And we will see enough of it to encourage us to believe that as a Democracy we are going to survive throughout all this tendency toward cheapening and the rise of mediocrity into high places.

The life of the village in America is the problem, the opportunity and the privilege of the architect: to devise a house that is not an imitation of a city house. We have to consider a radical change in the location of the house. We have got to have more ground for it. We have got to stop this huddling along a thoroughfare. Or if we are going to build along the thoroughfare, we should learn from the better countries and regions of Europe where they recognize the street and then develop a home ground behind and around the house. Where if there is a picture window it looks upon something beside the street. I imagine the old days of the street procession, where the king came along with his courtiers, and the big shows in the streets. Everybody then all came out in the front when the procession passed by, and his highness bowed and had great benefit from an occasion.

We don't have that any more, and if we do have it, it isn't worth very much. It is worth a lot more to live pleasantly, richly, with a sense of beauty. Now after all what "pays off" best in all this look back that you can take upon history? What have we got today? What has been preserved for us either in religion or in society or even in government?

The thing that was beautiful, the thing people felt had true beauty, was what survived. Today there is no preservation of anything that was not a consequence of its beauty at the time. And we attempt to preserve the beauty that existed at that time. So beauty pays off. Beauty survives, and out of that came the old saw that we have, that "all passes—art alone survives." The thought is true. What you can make beautiful is what will remain, and what is not beautiful will pass away. I see no possibility for beauty in quantity.

The only possibility for beauty lies in the emphasis on and development of the quality of individuality in everything you do. It has a tremendous reservoir of possibilities and privileges, hardly touched upon by any philosophy we have had previously.

(June 14, 1953)

THE REST OF THE WORLD

England

You have heard of the A.A. of England: the A.A. is the Architectural Association of Britain. It is the official architectural school of the nation, consisting of some five hundred students now—too many. It is 105 years old this year. So it is very old and very respectable, on Bedford Square, where it has outgrown all its buildings and built a building behind. Some bombs fell not far in the back and they have rebuilt a temporary shed there in which I saw all the students working on projects that were absolutely dead as a nit—had no quality and no character.

When we got to England, Jordan *[Robert Furneaux-Jordan, School Director]* was there with his car, the Daimler, and a chauffeur, and took us from Southhampton to London. We later drove through that historic country where George Meredith lived, Surrey, Sussex, through all these provincial towns which we have copied over here. It is a fact that you have to go to England really to discover this country. People who have lived here all their lives don't realize that everything here is aping everything over there—of the worst sort of the provincial type. It is the provincial English village that we got, not the beautiful English countryside village. We got provincial ugliness which characterizes the English to this day. And I don't think—so far as I can see—that we've done one thing to change it. Our towns, our villages, our streets, especially our eastern ones are ugly, provincial stuff.

The greatest surprise of all was the green that England puts forth—it makes our green look gray. The most vivid, living green you ever saw. It is everywhere, along the roads, throughout England. In the past the farmers, sheep raisers, cattle raisers, drove their herds to market, so there was a law passed so that there would be a grazing strip left beside the roads, where the flocks and herds, as they drove them to market, could graze as they went. That grazing strip has now become a wonderful growth of trees, shrubs, flowers, foliage. So everywhere you go in England, you drive through magnificent forested lanes. I never heard about that—never saw it before. You see through them occasionally, these beautifully managed landscapes—there are no fences, hedges everywhere, beautifully tilled fields.

And when we got to the old English architecture—Camden or the Cotswold hills or those places—we found it was very much like our stuff in proportion and feeling. It belonged there, not only belonged there, it belonged to the people who lived in it. It had evidently been done with love, and some depth of feeling that was missed when the provincials came over here. Now probably it was the inferior element who came over here—who quit, the unsuccessful element. So the charm of English countryside life and architecture was missed by us here when we established our architecture. Well, that's something that was a great surprise to me.

Then came London. We got there and we had a quaint little hotel out there in Kensington that had been built 125 years ago and was still just as it was. They didn't have very good service, but the old atmosphere was there, and quiet. It was on Queensgate Terrace, not far from the palace, the heart of London, but quiet as could be. And across, rows of houses that you see in Philadelphia, that you see all over our country. Rows of intensely respectable houses with little porches out in front; every house the same porch, and two columns standing up, holding a little entablature, and then the front door about four feet in. And those little porches all along, badges of respectability, no meaning at all. And they went up six stories, some of them, behind the roof dormers, counting the basement as one story.

There was miles of that in London but, with all of it, the whole aspect of London is so much richer and pleasanter and human-like and strongly built, firmly established; you get a sense of establishment that seems impregnable. It seems that it has been there forever, and always will be. Green breaking through it everywhere—parks, yards overflowing with green. Flowers everywhere, and nothing straight and dull, nothing rectangular in the place. It was a great and pleasant surprise to see this great city in the world so habitable. Somehow they had succeeded in making London habitable to an extreme. I understood what Dr. Johnson meant when he said that he loved London because every man was so close to his borough. And it seems practically so. Within a block or two or three you can find everything you could ever want. There will be a theater, a cinema, a dry goods store, a barber, a turkish bath—you couldn't think of anything that wouldn't be within reach almost anywhere in London.

Well, it's an amazing creation in the name of a city. And when you get to New York, you see these great masses of buildings and arid pavements enclosing this one rectangular park—Central Park—and nothing. When we got to Southhampton, I was astonished to see what they had rebuilt. To see those magnificent cranes—hundreds of them—for handling shipping, and ships themselves in dry docks and great new, almost a mile long, well constructed sheds—not sheds, they were really edifices. And when you got to New York there was a frightful contrast—that shabby waterfront of New York that is terrible to look at. New York seemed dirty in comparison to all this freshness, what with everybody painting, England sprucing up.

And Bedford Square, this ancient Square, is where the bombs had dropped close by but hadn't hit the Square. And they hadn't hit the school except in the rear; and of course I had to go down and look at the boys' work to see what they were doing. I didn't see anything worth giving a prize to. So I said to Jordan, who was a very intelligent and pretty wise shepherd, "Why do you give them prizes, when they haven't earned it, they haven't deserved it. Why do you issue these prizes?" "Well," he said, "they have been gifts from various sources to this enterprise, and of course we have to give them." And I handed them out when the occasion came.

They built a tent in Bedford Square that would hold 800 people, and there they had this assembly of very nice looking audience, beautiful, finely dressed and as well conditioned an audience as you've ever seen. The light played through on the canvas from the trees overhead very much as it does in Arizona. It was very beautiful.

(August 6, 1950)

France

Frank Lloyd Wright rarely spoke of France, and the selection that follows is typically slight but worth including if only because of its opening lines.

In France you have had a substitute for souls; your substitute is delicacy. France, do not lose the grace of your touch, do not be misled by a frightened people that count on its fingers freedoms up to four because they do not know freedom. Freedom's secret is within the spirit, and notwithstanding Napoleon, the luster of France does not lie in the harsh glare of militarism but lives in her own genius, in the love of reason of her philosophers and the beauty of her poets. France really lived when she lined up on the side of freedom, equality and fraternity—a lesson learned from the forefathers of the United States of America but which those states now seem in danger of forgetting. Oh France, put your trust in your native genius. Internationalism is good only when preserving what is French in France, Italian in Italy, British in Britain, Russian in Russia, and it consists in appreciation by each and every nation of what constitutes the soul of the other, and insists on uniting for the protection of that individuality.

(March 9, 1952)

Italy

Italy is the heart, really, if not the soul of all we call architecture, music and painting. And when you see Italy, when you see the fields as you see in Umbria—you see them all through Italy for that matter, but particularly in Umbria—you see how cultivation, tillage, is architecture. How it makes a pattern, and how carefully, how imaginatively they treat everything they do. Then you look at the buildings and they belong to the tillage, and the tillage and the buildings are of course part of the ground. It is all one beautiful harmony with a synthesis, I think, that exists nowhere in the world except in China and Japan. I suppose it did exist in Persia in ancient times. It never did exist in India. But there even in Italy today it isn't spoiled. Nothing really has damaged it except the Renaissance itself.

It was when they got classic architecture that they began to destroy the simplicity and beauty of their own heart-built and heart-felt art. It wasn't true of painting, it wasn't true of music. But it was true of architecture because they went over to the columns, and the things that went with them, the pilaster, the cornice, the entablature, and all that. And that destroyed the heart-architecture of Italy. They know it now, they feel it and they see it themselves.

I think that of our work there was hardly a building there that wouldn't look well in Italy—in old Italy, not in Renaissance Italy. There is a wonderful sympathy between the architecture we are turning out and the architecture of old Italy and they feel it. And I think the depth of our appreciation and our welcome in Italy was due to the fact that they feel it—and they said so. They gave us a wonderfully warm, heart-felt recognition. In spite of all the ceremonies and decorative pomp and glory, there was a heart in it all. It all came through in that fashion, which was immensely touching and convincing and all the rest of it.

The Italian heart is really the heart of the creative artist and the creative mind. It is a little confused, politically, now. Mussolini did them a great deal of harm. While he espoused modern ideas, he did it without knowing the nature of them. I heard of the railway station in Rome as a great piece of modern architecture. I went to see it and found it to be infected with the same grandomania that had characterized the Renaissance. It was out of scale, it wasn't good at all. On the contrary the railway station in Florence is one of the finest pieces of modern architecture I have ever seen, with some feeling for proportion that is human and in human scale. It is not grandomania. And most of the Italian modern work is in human scale. But where Mussolini went he seems to have done the bad thing in the bad way.

The Vatican when I first saw it—hadn't seen it since 1910, that's forty-one years ago—then the beautiful forecourt of the Vatican with that curved arcade was open to the city. Mussolini built a lot of commonplace buildings right in front of it, cutting it off from the city. I can't see that he did one single thing that didn't hurt Rome. But we came through Rome rather fast—didn't stay long, because it was depressing to me, seemed something like a vast graveyard. The graveyard of something that hadn't come to life again and never can come. That's why this effort of Mussolini's, so ill advised, was aborted, because they can't shake off the weight of that old grandomania. But when we got to Florence, the whole thing changed, the heart came through again.

I don't think there is any manifest heart of Italy in Rome today. I don't think you'd find it anywhere, least of all in Michelangelo's Vatican. Rather amusing that our guest on the excursion, Lloyd Lewis' wife Catherine, got to wearing shorter and shorter sleeves until her shoulder points were showing when we showed up at the Vatican. And she was barred by the arm of the guard and kept out of it because she had too much flesh showing. She is a good Catholic, too. It shows how the old rituals and the old struggle against animality is still maintained on a very bad and useless basis. We did not see the Pope, but we did meet our own ambassador and he sent us up from Rome to Florence in a motor car. And that's how we saw Assisi.

Assisi was St. Francis' baliwick, and it is in the heart of Umbria midway between Florence and Rome. That's the part of Italy, if you ever get a chance to go, that I advise you to see. Go to Umbria, go to Assisi, and if you can afford it, stay at the Hotel Baglioni. You might as well be warned that the prices you pay in Europe now are just about the same as New York City at the Plaza or any other of the swell hotels. This dollar of ours has seemed to wake up the world to standards which they are quite willing to accept where we are concerned. Where they are concerned, I think they make concessions. If we are going to boost the standard we have got to take the consequences—and we do.

In Florence we saw the damage the Germans had done for spite as they were leaving. They had mined the bridges across the Arno and touched them all off except one—the Ponte Vecchio is still there. The others are rubble. They are rebuilding the Trinity bridge, which is a beautiful bridge. Florence doesn't really seem to be damaged to any appreciable extent. There was the old Palazzo Vecchio, the old Square, all the old things that I was familiar with forty-one years ago—haven't changed a hair. After all, forty-one years doesn't seem to be very long in the architectural world. Just sort of a brief day. But that's where it began, that's where they began to feel it. The teacher of the architectural university in Sicily brought about thirty-one of his pupils, half boys and half girls clear up just to shake hands. Sat in the lobby of the hotel for about twenty minutes, and then they went back the way they had come.

Venice was a wonderful experience, and of course it is the greatest sight, picturesquely, in all Italy. We didn't stay very long or see very much of it, but you don't have to drink a tub of dye to know what color it is. And there it was—I think that's the place we would like to go back to for a vacation some day. Venice is really beautiful. There you see the thing we talked about a moment ago. You see the old Ducal Palace, which is one of the loveliest buildings on earth, right out of the heart of old Italy, and then next to it Sansovino's marvelously contrived and exquisitely academic facade.

There you see from then on what you'll see throughout Italy, and all through Europe. You see the Renaissance eating into the old native buildings, the Renaissance destroying the facades of the old cathedrals, as it did in Milan, and as it does everywhere. When the Italians took over the Gothic, they made it gay. They missed entirely the spirit of the Gothic, as it was conceived by the Goths. They wanted to make it light and cheerful and charming, and they did it in Venice. They did it in Milan also, in that cathedral. That is the only one that starts to be efflorescent right at the ground and keeps it up to the finish in the center. So the Italians had that light, deft, gay touch on everything.

The day of the old troubadors, when music was everywhere in the public streets and where costume was something—we saw a little of it in the ceremony in the Palazzo Vecchio. Gaiety, extraordinary elaboration of the personal element, individuality too, rampant. There was no style, much. I don't think the Italians in their native life ever subscribed to a uniform style. They all built out of themselves, dressed out of themselves, sang out of themselves, and that's why it is so peculiar a joy to be taken to the heart of Italy. After this, I think there is nothing we can have that is going to move us very deeply. Everything from now on will probably be post-mortem, anti-climax.

The show [Sixty Years of Living Architecture, at the Palazzo Strozzi in Florence] is as remarkable as it was in Philadelphia and even more so. Because it occupied twenty-one rooms in the Palazzo Strozzi, and each is a little show in itself. When you go through the doorway, from room to room to room—all have this vaulted ceiling coming down, resting on corbels, wonderfully dignified atmosphere—you think at first that the scale of our performance would be overwhelmed by the situation. But it isn't. Stonorov [Oscar Stonorov organized the show] managed the start of it very nicely by putting in a low, red-paneled ceiling which you enter under. And you feel it clear through the show after that, giving you the scale like a yardstick, so that you hold it and keep it all through the twenty-one rooms of the palace. And of course it is well done in every respect. . . .

Go and see Italy. You needn't bother about the rest of it, because when you have seen Italy you have seen the origin of everything else. All you see when you see the other countries is what they did with it, which isn't very creditable to them. You see the best adaptations in Spain; you see the worst probably in England and Germany. The next worst would be in France. France has the first version of the little gold medal with the *fleur-de-lis,* which was the mark of old Florence for a century before Francis I came over there to get workmen to go to France to do the work. And you can easily see that the French *fleur-de-lis* was originally Florentine. And as it was with that, so it was with nearly everything that they do. I doubt if you can find a thing in France before the advent of Baron Hausmann's mansard that was not Italian. The mansard roof was not Italian. That was the French contribution to the architecture of the world—the mansard roof. Now England did make a contribution of her own in a certain homeliness in the older, better periods of her architecture. She did have a sense of comfort and of the adaptation of architecture to human uses and needs that is very nice and very good practise—something to be admired. But in the French version, I think nothing.

Soon came the Baroque, soon came the efflorescence, soon came the degeneracy that wiped it all out. It came by way of the French, mostly, the Germans following in, hellbent for election. Probably Spain preserved most of its original flavor, but to get back—when you hitchhike around the world, why just start in Italy and take it all in. You can forget all the rest until you get to the Orient. There it will begin again.

(July 8, 1951)

Japan

This selection explores Japan from the inside as it were, by delineating the Japanese spirit through its art, specifically some nineteenth century prints by Hiroshige, and by comparing and contrasting that spirit with our own.

That's a typical Japanese scene by the roadside *[Frank Lloyd Wright is showing Hiroshige prints]*. Those little signs are everywhere. See the little bird perched on it? And you always see these coolies warming their behinds before the fire along the roadside in big groups, wherever you go. There they are fording the river. That's the *daimeo [feudal lord]* himself with the cargo there, being ferried across by the professional ferrymen.

And this is a scene along the early stages—crossing the Yokohama fields. This was a block that was lost and subsequently recut many times— once by Hiroshige himself, and then by Aesi. Sometimes these blocks would crack and be ruined for printing—in which case they would cut another, never just the same.

Now, you see, the perfection of these makes these earlier ones look rather thin. But that very thinness has a simplicity that has an artistic value. Now they indicate rain—this is a slight summer rain—the sky is still golden, but you see evening is coming on. You see how they indicate the rain? It's abstract. When you once start with these prints, you never look at nature the same way after. You never have the scene quite the same way as other people who are looking at it who haven't seen these things. A certain natural selection and arrangement takes place in your own sense of the thing as you look. Certain realistic things disappear, and the whole scene becomes more effective and simple because you know this art— that's the effect it has on you. It can cultivate your sensibilities where landscape is concerned—or your seeing anything.

Do you notice how this man sees? He doesn't see the way our Western artists see at all. He doesn't see the same thing. His chiaroscuro, you see, is not there. He has these substitutes for it—this, what we call *noton [a half tone method to produce light and shade]*, is a substitute for chiaroscuro. But the ordinary Western painter would just deluge that thing without regard to surface. There would be no surface. But in all these the surface is preserved as surface beautifully. So they become patterns. They really are, in spite of their being perfect delineations of the scene. They are abstract, and they do have a certain convention which they keep to absolutely. The young pine forest growing up on the hillside—the strolling players in the center—the village top over there in the vistas.

Now here is one of the Japanese heroes—a great wrestler; probably famous all over the Empire, being carried across by coolies on a horse. They lead the horse across the water. Usually his lady is with him—is she there? Here she is. There is a building going on to the right, a characteristic Japanese bridge to the left. That's Nagoya, I should think, by the fish terminals of the roofs. These are all actual places. And the trees are moved a little, and some of the trees are gone, but actually at the time these were portraits of those places. This was about a hundred years ago. Of course, great changes have taken place during that time, and some of these places themselves have disappeared, but I've checked on some of them and substantially they are like the prints.

Now their horses—before I'd seen Japan, I thought how funny the horses looked. And the horses are funny, just like that. They aren't the same as our horses. And have you noticed in all these landscapes, there is no blending, no beach, there is no declension from shore to water. You see Japan has submerged in all these years, so the water comes sharp up on everything. It's abrupt. There are no gentle slopes to the shoreline anywhere. There is just water striking solid ground. You'll notice that in these prints.

That one's a very full, rich print in color. They are not often as rich as that. Some tastes would choose this print, some would prefer a lighter one. That's the kind of atmosphere you see perpetually, not only in Japan, but in Arizona, Phoenix. That's the Japanese rendering of the waves— isn't that interesting. It's more sheer, more definitely sheer, than the Westerner would ever have presented it.

Now here's the thing I was talking about—the water coming up— that looks as if it had sunk, and it has. There is no beach, no shoreline there. But this is the sky I first saw when we first came into Yokohama harbor, rose all over, beautiful golden sky. And I saw Fujiyama just like that, in the distance there—white against the sky. And I saw these little white sampans you see in the next picture—hundreds of them, literally thousands of them, all around. Just little white specks on the horizon—it's a beautiful thing.

(September 20, 1950)

America and Ancient Sumer

This pride we take in organic architecture is just as natural, would be absolutely natural, to the Sumerians. I think it would be the ideal in, surely, what they did. Didn't they do the ziggurat? What's more organic than the ziggurat? And they had all the sciences that we have today that we gloat over. I dare say that if there was any space ship needed at that time—of course they weren't so much in need of the space ship then—but if they had needed one I think they would have invented one.

And when I saw that wonderful collection of Sumerian relics in Baghdad, and the old curator was very kind and went around with us several times explaining everything, I saw how the Greeks were merely moderns and modernistic—that's the word I want. The Greeks were modernistic, because the Sumerians had done almost everything in the way of architecture and sculpture, gold working, ornamentation, better than the Greeks ever did it. Something was gone when the Greeks took the thing they did, I saw a harp that they had done a more beautiful thing in itself imaginable—a musical instrument invented by the Sumerians, the birthday of civilization.

Now if we could only have proceeded according to the birthright of civilization, think where we might be now instead of where we are, confused and virtually terror stricken wherever an idea appears. We are afraid of ideas. We are afraid of the men who swear by them and who dedicate their lives to them, and as a matter of fact, we ridicule dedication of any kind, don't we? Whereas the Sumerian civilization was in itself a dedication. And with great understanding and enthusiasm they developed a great art, a great architecture and undoubtedly therefore, a great life—although what we have in the way of remains of the philosophy of that period then more beautiful than the carving. It's very like the Egyptian, of course, only more compact, more simple, and more beautiful. And there you'll find almost all the maxims and all of the wisdom later recorded by the Egyptian scrolls and by the various things that came afterward.

So somehow it's when an idea is fresh, when it first appears it has its great impress, its great effect. Then gradually it becomes absorbed and this feature of it appears there, and that feature appears somewhere else, and it becomes absorbed into the life of the time and its origin lost. Which is all right. But what I started to say was that only an idea, so far as we have any ability to discern the truth, never dies. This phase of it'll appear there and that phase of it'll appear here, but it goes on. And the fact that Sumeria had the same crack, and that I have enjoyed, and that many people have enjoyed because of me, and other people must have it too, I don't think it could be original with me—shows how in the stream of consciousness it's all there, and all waiting to be rediscovered, maybe, felt again, projected again and again and again and again, almost as our features are.

I don't think the Sumerian features as I saw them were a bit different from those of ours today. Their beards, their headdress, and the beautiful gold ornaments that they contrived for headdresses I've never seen equaled, by the Greeks or by anybody else. Beautiful thin plates of gold put together with little, what do you call them, on the head hanging down over the ears. And they would take the back and do something beautiful with it. And when you put one of those on you're really king-like, or queen-like as you like. And [the woman] sitting with that golden headdress playing the harp that I saw couldn't leave very much to be desired.

And if we could do as well today... what's the matter with us anyhow? Why can't we? What's gone out? Have we lost the simple motivation of beauty that was originally in our birth, that we were born with? Why is it that now everything is confused and awkward and unrelated to the spirit and has no spiritual verification to give us in the name of beauty? Have we been too numerous, are there too many of us now? Have we become ordinary by way of number? Or have we lost something essential in the way of primitive life, the primitive values of life, the special ordination that seemed to be a part of being born in the days when humanity was more scarce.

Well anyhow, it's a dubious subject, and not treated upon very intelligently, so far as I know. But I know perfectly well that all that is of great strength and virtue now, always was, and nothing new has occurred. Except as we re-perceive—except as we again—something, somehow breaks through the gradual veil that has drawn over the human perception, grown over the human individual to make him complex. See his clothes today. See how many pieces it takes to dress him. And then look at the Sumerian dress, beautifully adapted to the statuesque nobility of the human figure, men and women, simple and related directly. You are all familiar with that note the poor artistic gentlemen left when he committed suicide. He said he was tired of all this buttoning and unbuttoning. I think it's that buttoning and unbuttoning that's the matter with us. I think we have to button and unbutton everything. Nothing comes naturally free and clear to human use and consciousness. And when we do see a little of that simplicity, we still—and when I say we I mean those who make a life study of it and are devoted to it—can see by a flash of intuition perhaps or something still living in us, that that's the way and that's beautiful.

(December 28, 1958)

Frank Lloyd Wright and Mayor Richard J. Daley, at Frank Lloyd Wright Day Banquet, Chicago, October 17, 1956

At the Guggenheim Museum construction site, 1957

Frank Lloyd Wright and Herbert F. Johnson (at left) at Johnson Tower construction site, 1948

Broadacre City model, detail section, 1934

Frank Lloyd Wright and Sir Clough Williams-Ellis, Portmeirion, Wales, 1956

Frank Lloyd Wright and architect Carlo Scarpa, Venice, 1951

Frank Lloyd Wright and the first class to graduate from his building at the Jiyu Gakuen School of the Free Spirit, Tokyo, Japan, 1921

Ando Hiroshige (1797-1858): from the series "Thirty-Six Views of Mount Fuji," 1858

ARCHITECTURE AND
THE ARTS

Where Part Three dealt with the world of Frank Lloyd Wright, this Part comprises what for him was the universe—architecture, the alpha and the omega. If God existed for him other than as Nature with a capital N, it was as master architect whose handiwork was infinite. And as God created a structure for His universe, so he felt man must by his own efforts create timeless structures to live in.

Like Part One, Autobiography, Part Four is all of a piece, reflecting how architecture for Frank Lloyd Wright was, like his life, a seamless continuity. For him the nature of his art involved soul and mind as well as craftsmanship, and also what he termed "discipline," that form of obligation which distinguishes the noble from the common. At the end of his life he was working on a book for children, *The Wonderful World of Architecture,* that extolled the same principles which distinguished him at the very outset of his career. Nothing had changed, only deepened and expanded. And here, as he talks about architecture and the arts, about architecture and other cultures, he confirms on all fronts the message that "The main fact about an architect is that he is a poet. And that poetry of his is more or less connected with religious experience. And if it isn't in the nature of a religious experience, he hasn't got it, and the best thing for him to do is to quit trying without that spirit, and go to work somewhere and try to do something else. Because to be a creative architect is to cultivate the poetic spirit and to understand what it means and its relation to what is called God. It's all one thing, and nothing is insignificant concerning it."

Toward the making of an architect there are lessons to be learned, from theory, through observation, and by means of those technical aspects which give tangible reality to all the rest. The making of an architect, therefore, must teach what architecture means, how it functions, what materials it uses, and the world of nature it is to inhabit. Then on to the act of creation itself, wherein the architect will "become the pencil in the hand of the infinite," ordering his little world as God orders His universe, learning the definitions of that world and how they work: tenuity, which enables one to push and pull on the structure; the unit system, a grid drawn on the plan itself.

Finally we arrive at actual construction, of a one-room house and of a state capitol for Arizona—this last a remarkable talk in which we literally "see" the creation of a building taking place. After those creations Part Four ends as Frank Lloyd Wright would surely have wished it, with a view toward the future, where "eventually we are going to have the greatest architecture and the greatest sense of art in life that ever existed in the world."

The Nature of Art

If Beethoven, sitting down to the piano to compose a sonata, or even a scherzo, were to imitate the sounds of nature which had inspired and interested him, and you heard the gander gandering and the birds twittering and all of the sounds that you are familiar with in the barnyard in his opus, you wouldn't regard him very highly as an artist, would you? I don't think you would. But if, out of the music which he made for you, inspired by that phase of nature, it was recalled to you in a pleasurable way according to the circumstances in which you were, and in which music is made, then you see a process of digestion would have taken place in the artistic performance—in the artist's mind. It would have passed through this alembic that is called the soul, and would have come to you in the terms of music. In the terms of even the violin it would have to be different from the piano, and the flute different from the violin and the piano. He would have to have been master of those mediums, violated none of them, and made you think of these things.

Now that's the difference between a work of art and a work of a lower category. Now you will find it all through the fabric of the world you're going to inhabit. You'll find degrees of it. You'll see paintings, you'll see things that are just about as far off the beam as you dare go and stay on it. Then you'll see other things that are, frankly, to hell with the beam. And you get a certain pleasure out of that too, perhaps, but only temporarily. You wouldn't want to live with it, or own it, or even if you were an artist yourself, acknowledge it; but you might be amused by it.

Now, we seem to have touched upon something here that I thought would become more evident than it seems to be. What we are finally landing on is the line of demarcation between the work of nature and the work of art. Now a work of art is a work of nature, but it is a work of human nature. It is a work of the mind: and it's a work of the mind in circumstances for an occasion which, to which, for which, and in which it may be supremely natural and simple and effective. But to take the thing as it was in the first place as a work of nature, and exploit it? No. Now you can go far with that exploitation and that is really what we see most of when you see these attempts now being made in modern art. When you see the pictures that are being painted, when you see these youngsters and oldsters going out and sitting there and performing, very few of them really know what they are doing. And very few of them come in with a beautiful interpretation of what they have seen. They'll come in with one phase or another of exploitation of that thing.

Now think about it, and the thing will begin to come clear, and it will straighten out for you a great deal that is terribly confused now in the world of art, especially in the world of painting, because their things are so easy to do. In architecture too, but then it's more difficult, very hard to do. In architecture particularly and peculiarly you are more disciplined by the nature of your calling, by the nature of your effort, than any of the other arts are, unless it is music. Perhaps music is . . . the composer in music is disciplined as severely as the architect. But the painter knows no discipline. And that's why when I was a child I was not allowed to draw from nature until I had mastered the principles and elements that made the appearances that were lying around on the surface what they were. And it was the composition of those appearances, and the elements of geometry inevitable to them, that made them what they were, that I was to become familiar with. And then I could intelligently render the characteristics of what I saw in the medium that I might choose to render it in—either painting or music or sculpture or architecture. Do you see the point? That's not subtle. That's all the difference between architecture and the realm of imitation which you might call monkey business.

(December 19, 1954)

"The Wonderful World of Architecture"

On his return from Baghdad to the United States in the spring of 1957 Frank Lloyd Wright stopped in London to meet with the publishers of Rathbone Press. They were putting out a series of illustrated books, primarily for children, under the rubric The Wonderful World of. . . . *They contracted with Mr. Wright for a book on architecture. He was working on the manuscript at the time of his death.*

The title and format of the book leads me to believe that it is for children. It is primarily for either the precocious child or the hindered adult. Mrs. Wright said that to the man who published the book, and he didn't like it.

It has to be simple, direct to the point. They wanted to start it with the architecture of the animals. But architecture to me doesn't lie there. That's the underworld of architecture. You don't have legitimate architecture until the mind of man takes hold with a desire for beauty which is to him an acquisition. To the animal it is of course natural. It's a gift from nature to the animal to build beautifully, like the tortoise shell, for instance, or like so many instances of beautiful markings and patterns. Look at your rattlesnakes, look at nearly everything nature has gifted: the seashells on the shore, there you see housing. And housing according to instinct.

Man's architecture is not according to his instinct. Somehow or other he was not given the gift of housing himself beautifully, because at first he inhabited caves. He was a cave dweller with a big club and hair all over his body. Out of that there has had to come this thing we call architecture by way of man's spirit, of his desire to live beautifully and to know the beautiful and to construct it and leave it on earth as a memento of his own power and value. Now that's architecture.

So I'm not beginning this book, except casually, with instinctive building. I'm making a distinct difference between conscious architecture built to be beautiful by the mind of man and the lower orders of the same thing, which are instinctive and a gift. The question is, does man have that same instinct, lower down? And can you see in his constructions, when he wants to build, a similar gift from nature to that of the animals? It's a moot point, but at least you can't call it architecture. You call it building. Building becomes architecture only when the mind of man consciously takes it and tries with all his resources to make it beautiful, to put concordance, sympathy with nature, and all that into it. Then you have architecture.

(February 22, 1959)

The Architect As Poet

Architecture isn't something that you get out of magazines and books, or even learn about from architects themselves. It's something that is a living spirit all the while present in you and in everything you do. It can be cultivated consciously, and that's our job. That's what we mean; that's what we're here for, and if we allow ourselves to live in an ugly way, if we promote excesses and if we get things jumbled up and discordant, all that is unbecoming to your spirit as an architect. And an architect is a poet, you know.

The main fact about an architect is that he is an artist, and the main fact concerning an artist is that he is a poet. And that poesy of his is more or less connected with religious experience. And if it isn't in the nature of a religious experience with him, he hasn't got it, and the best thing for him to do is to quit trying. Without that spirit he'd better go to work somewhere and try to do something else. Because to be a creative architect is to cultivate the poetic spirit and to understand its relation to what is called God. It's all one thing, and nothing is insignificant concerning it. That's where the architect is the reminder to his fellow beings of what constitutes their virtue. So you are all young advocates along that line, and the way that we live here should be exemplary. We can't afford to let it down.

(August 22, 1954)

Architecture and Music

It seems to me that music is a kind of sublimated mathematics. So is architecture a kind of sublimated mathematics, and in the same sense. There lies the great relationship and warm kinship between music and architecture. They require very much the same mind. A Beethoven's mind would be that of a great architect's mind. His thinking process was a building process. It was a proceeding from generals to particulars along a specific scheme with a particular idea, and then building, building, building, building a great edifice of sound.

My father was the man who taught me to regard a symphony as an edifice of sound. And when he told me that, I may have been ten years old. I began to listen to music as a kind of building. And that is why I like Beethoven so much, because I could see Beethoven build. If you take Beethoven's sonatas—that is when he was at his highest intellectual and probably spiritual reach, when he was designing a sonata—they were manifestly things for the mind as well as for feeling. And in all those sonatas you will find him building, designing, constructing with marvelous finesse and with marvelous structural ability. That is also an architect's work.

(August 27, 1952)

The Making of an Architect

Before the twentieth century, architects had little regard for the true nature of materials. This use of materials in accordance with their most fitting attributes was one of the first things Frank Lloyd Wright taught us.

I think we ought to talk this morning to the newcomers. They must have something turning over in their minds concerning where they are and how they are. Won't some of you boys start the ball rolling— something you want to know about that you think I might be able to answer. Sixty-five years in architecture with both hands ought to be a qualification for something or other, if only the abandonment of the game.

How many of you have built buildings yourselves? Even if it was a chicken house?

Apprentice: Well, I helped.

One. Well then, you're all fresh, all have your feet on the path and I trust with a good pair of shoes. Did it ever occur to you what the nature of architecture is, which you've chosen for your life's work? What is architecture? I had this young group of Neutra's in here the other day and pulled my favorite confuser on them. And it was perfectly successful, not one of them knew. I said, "Do you know what a good translation in English would be of the name you're going to wear all the rest of your lives?" No answer. And I put it a little more simply because they were foreigners, and still no answer. I'm putting it to you now. What is, would be, a good translation of the word "architect"?

What is and who is an architect, and how and why is he? You must know, you boys, you look so intelligent to me. No answer. Well, the word "arch," in the sense that it's in architecture, means like the archbishop, means the top, the arch, the high one, the one above all the others. Then "tech" of course you know the meaning of; that's technology, technique, "tech," like the Toltecs. "Tech" means the know-how, means how to put things together. So that the proper translation of the word "architect" is the "master of the know-how." Isn't that a good translation? Well, that's what you are eager to be, masters of the know-how. And what's the know-how? Isn't the structure of everything there is, geology, chemistry, anything that nature has produced by way of form, isn't that architecture? Then isn't nature your best schoolbook? What other book could compare with direct reading into the nature for the construction of the universe? And you're a part of that universe, along with all the disagreeable objects that occupy the earth, and the agreeable and beautiful ones.

To begin at the beginning, where do you go to study? Where do you get your information? From books? No, because very few of the fellows who wrote the books ever began at the beginning. They read other books and compiled ideas from other ideas and tried to sift them down to a conclusion that would be according to what they wanted to see themselves. But if you begin at the beginning, you begin with nature, and with the interior study of nature. Until after a while you begin to look at things for their picturesque qualities and values. And looking at them is what may intrigue and interest you to look into them. All the information that you as an architect are going to receive is to look into the thing which you are looking at. And what are you looking for when you're looking in? The nature of that thing, how it came to be as it is, what its characteristics are, what the difference is between a stone and a brick and a board. And when you master that elementary sense of materials. You become the prophet of those materials, you prophesy them when you build and use them, because you use them according to their nature.

Anything used according to its nature in the category of organic architecture is beautiful; it truly is. A brick is a very simple thing, you know. Just rectangular, but it has a great range of quality. And your sense of quality, your ability to distinguish it, determines whether you are going to be a good architect or not. Whether you can see the beauty of a brick and use it in such a way that one beauty of that brick becomes infinitely more beautiful—so that nobody knew a brick could look so well. And that's true of stone and it's true of wood also. So it's out of the interior nature of all these things that you really get your materials for building.

Now when you get to the building, there again, what is the nature of the problem? First off, what is this building to be? Is it a chicken house, a palace, a memorial, or just a good time place? Now what would constitute the nature of that purpose? How would you best render it by being master of all these other qualities, and adding them up, and using them according to their nature? You could really produce something significant, you see. Now if what you did was not significant, you might better never have done it, so far as your being an architect is concerned, because it merely encumbers the earth. But if it is significant and prophetic, then you're on the road to being an architect. And you indeed have the quality of mind that will eventuate into a soul capable of expression, capable of expressing the nature of the human soul. And you will have arrived at the conclusion that architecture is essentially human, and with human values.

When you become a master of those values you're pretty well on the road to being a prophetic architect. You'll know how to build what, and where. I would say, that where is less important than what. But where is important. The nature of the site on which you build should help determine, in a well-considered design, the shape of things to come.

Well, you see anybody can become an architect who goes deep enough and honestly enough into the nature of things. Now technique, that is something else. It is pitiful to see how all of the expert knowledge which has been accumulated in the name of technique by our engineers and our architects has absolutely missed the point until organic architecture began to appear. In organic architecture you can't miss the point.

Here we are with all the new materials that came in. Here comes steel, we'll say. Now all the old materials were here, weren't they? We had bricks, stone, wood, but we didn't have steel. Steel is an artificial product. Steel is really a plastic, a ductile thing. It has tenuity. That's its chief value. Now if you boys, in your study of nature, had been really there at the time steel appeared, you would have analyzed steel. You would have seen that its strength lay in its capacity to be drawn out thin and pull tremendous loads. That is, tenuity was its chief characteristic, and studied it was tremendously effective.

The engineers of the past had no such view, and if they had, they had no technique to go with it. So the steel companies furnished steel to the architects, and the engineers rolled the steel into lumber. Steel lumber became the basis for all nineteenth century architecture. And it has held well over into the middle of the twentieth, with just a sign now of beginning to understand that steel is tenuity, not lumber. So here we are getting a new view of an old material. Now if we'd had organic knowledge on the part of the architects in that day we wouldn't have had to go through all this we've now got to go through. Because all these buildings you see standing in New York City and all through the country, these vaunted skyscrapers, are all steel framed lumber buildings. They are not modern structures according to the nature of steel.

Now I'm merely mentioning this to show how important it is that you get straight in your minds the character and the nature of the materials you use in order to know how to use them. When Roebling came in with his [Brooklyn] bridge, that was the first gigantic expression of the quality of steel in tension. When I built the Imperial Hotel I felt that pull was the nature of steel, and by way of that pull I could beat the 'quake. And I did. Even to this day that building is rocking to and fro. Ed Stone was in it the other day and told me that an earthquake came and he got scared and wanted to run out, and he saw that the boys were all going about their work as though nothing had happened and laughing at the fears expressed by the guests. So he sort of decided to stay. And he saw the columns tipping this way and that way, and the thing rolling through as though it was going to fall down or explode and in twenty minutes everything went back just as it was before.

That's the property of tenuity: tension, pull. And that property of pull never entered into a building by the ancients, you know. If the Greeks had had it, we wouldn't have had to do anything. They would have shown us how. Now we've got to learn how to use steel. And we've got to learn how to use glass. Glass was something that they didn't have either. Glass is air in air to keep air out or keep it in. No such thing ever happened in the world before. And when you take glass and steel together, there's your modern world. And there's your opportunity, fresh, new. The ancients can't help you solve it. The dome of St. Peter's won't help you. Nothing from the past will help you understand the nature of your new opportuniteis and your new fields.

(November 30, 1958)

Nature and Architecture

The place for an architect to study construction first of all, before he gets into the theory of the various formulas that exist in connection with steel beams, girders, and reinforced concrete, is the study of nature. In nature you will find everything exemplified, from the blade of grass to the tree, from the tree to the geological formations to the procession of eras beginning with the first from the sea downwards. And when you get a sense in your mind of that continuity and that elemental sense of process according to the nature of materials, you've got the basis for an architect's conceptions, for his practise, even.

When we are in Arizona there is no more profitable study in the world than to go out into the desert and see where, by necessity of the economy of materials, a marvelous scientific structure arises from God knows where—but you can see how, as in the saguaro cactus, for instance, or in any of the tubular forms that require a strong stalk against the wind and against attack. Everything in the desert has to be armed, because it has to preserve its existence by opposition to all other forms of life in the desert. So the saguaro grows these thorns and spikes not for fun, not just because it likes them, but because it has to have them in order to live.

You'll notice too the principle of nature that never shows any regard for anything in the way of economy. That's what makes the study of economy so artificial, so difficult, so fruitless, and in most cases so useless. When nature made these spikes, for instance, on the cactus, she didn't stop with just what was enough. She begin to like the idea of the spike, and a spike became spikes to such an extent that everything bristled all over and the bristles became very beautiful. And the more bristles there were, the more beautiful the thing became.

So nature has no regard for economy except—now here's a contradiction in terms—in order to get exuberance. She did economize on material in the stalk by using the lattice instead of the solid wall. But when it comes to these other expressions, even to the bloom which is way beyond anything you can conceive in these circumstances, the desert blossoms and takes on this prolific quality. And the spines, the spikes, the fences seem to be an inconsistency.

It is the study of nature in that sense that makes the ground work for wisdom of the architectural mind. It is not formed from books. It is not formed from theories. It is formed by keen observance of the processes, characteristics, and forms that take place around you, before you, everywhere. And as the conditions change, you will find all the forms changing. As the materials are called upon by nature to do certain things, and the results become evident, you'll see how form really does follow function. But that is the very least of the act. That's only the platform upon which these natural forces seem to operate and rest, because you will see this marvelous exuberance that is beauty. I remember William Blake said, "Exuberance is beauty." And I never understood what he meant. I thought that it was rather demoralizing and misleading until I began to see that what he meant was that everything as far as it can go in excess, according to nature, is good. Like the profusion of leaves on the tree, like the branch that puts out blossoms on a blossoming tree.

The more, the more richly, they are put forth, the more that is given, the more delight we take in the thing. All through nature you will find these propositions confronting you, and in their solution and study, and appreciation, and the love with which you take them in you will build up within yourselves a certain power, which is capable of judging quantities, effects, and proportions. I think perhaps from the study of nature in true sense, the most valuable thing you will get out of it is this sense of proportion. And you will not be afraid of exuberance, so long as that exuberance is in proportion and in character to the purpose of its origin.

So when you are told to study nature, that doesn't mean you are to go out and just look at the hills and the way the animals conduct themselves and what is visible on the surface. The study of nature means Nature with a capital N, Nature, inner nature, nature of the hand, of this apparatus, of this glass. The truth concerning all those things is architectural study, and the more you pursue it, the more that pursuit becomes you, the more your vision will become attuned to elemental things. And the more productive man you'll be in this field we call architectural design.

(June 28, 1953)

Desert Architecture

The structure of the saguaro cactus, which surrounds us on the Arizona desert, was an inspiration to Frank Lloyd Wright from the first time he saw it. The hollow interior, the vertical ribs carrying the exterior surface—like slender reinforcing rods—taught him valuable lessons from which he abstracted his own forms, both in the concrete block system he devised and in the tap-root foundation for his skyscraper designs.

This morning I think we ought to talk about our practical affairs here. Here we are in the desert again where everything is ready to fight everything else. Have you ever noticed—have you studied the cactus growths around here—how everything is armed not only to the teeth, but everywhere else? It's perfectly amazing, the economy, too, with which these things are built. If you want to study economy of construction, take a branch of, well, the saguaro is the limit, of course—and then you have the cholla. Have you boys ever examined a cholla stalk? You'll see them lying around here, all dried up. Nothing but the bones left—have you ever studied the bones of the cholla and see how the material is economized?

Now in the east that would grow solid. Around us in Wisconsin where things are all fat and easy you'd have a solid stalk with flesh. But up here you have this good pattern for reinforcing by steel. Here you have this strand, here you have all the scientific properties of steel construction evident in these things in the desert, where economy was imperative. And this saguaro has a skyscraper standing up, with just a little clutch at the bottom. Stands there all these years—have you ever seen one stripped? In each flute there is a rib, at that rib is *[fiber]* almost equal to steel. And it's all in tension, and all fastened down to a little root. And the root system is such that it's a marvel that it stands there at all. But it does, chiefly on account of its weight—great weight on a single point, you see. Then it has a little trunk root that goes like an elephant's trunk in search of water, and it will catch a little pool over here, probably, when it rains. The water will congregate there. Now it couldn't live on the water that it could get where it stands, so it goes out after water.

And you'll see all those simple, natural things that really are architecture and are engineering and everything else is based upon. Insofar as it's all natural like that, why, it's good. Then it all gets confused, and you get all sorts of reactionary, interactionary effects that work upon it that don't matter. So long as you stick to those elementary principles in architecture, it's all you need. No one needs to know how heavy you have to have, or knows the reactions in a beam—where it shall be six inch, eight inch channel, or a beam section—or that sort of thing. That's the book's knowledge that comes by being an engineer directly and professionally. But an architect doesn't need that. He has the engineer the way the engineer has the book. And he uses him that way. But he must know these elementary principles and reactions of nature.

And here you have a great chance to study them first hand. I know, I've been continually amazed, discovering new things as I walk around. You should take your walks daily, and go through and don't miss anything. Look at these little things around your feet. And you can see, of course, if you want, if you're interested geologically, you can see here the youngest country in this country—probably any other country—Arizona.

Arizona is very young. If you go further west you will see it gradually becoming smoother, more undulating, more quiet. But here it's tempestuous and freshly made. The cataclysm wasn't so far away, here. And of course all that you see in the way of nature here is cataclysmic.

It's the result of great explosive forces fighting each other, and what you see is a form of debris. But in that debris and the way it is left there and the way it's piled up, you can study all these things that constitute the nature of materials. You'll see them all there, and you'll also see the way nature has handled them.

And from that you also learn lessons. And what you should first get into your systems when you get here in the desert is to get that lesson from nature in architecture which is fundamental to the whole thing we call architecture. And here you have it stripped—in the east it's not so easy to come by. There is a great efflorescence. The difference between this bougainvillea and that cactus out there would be the difference between the two places; so in inhabiting the two places, you learn. You have the open book of nature. On the one page you have efflorescence, richness, ease, what comes of great. . . well I suppose actually it's a form of decay. Perhaps this vegetation that grows all over so abundantly is a form of mold that comes upon the more accurate elements—the stone foundation of things. But when you get out here, you're back to the foundation, and there you are to the process that goes somewhere.

No one has ever found out, or even prophesied I think yet whether the whole thing is degenerate or whether it is regenerate. We'd have to read that answer in the stars, wouldn't we. That's a species of cosmography. It concerns the architect, too. But to me an architect is a man who knows, first by nature, knows the secrets of nature and studies them, and is informed by them, and comes out strong with knowledge. He has a feeling first. At first he is an introvert and he gathers all this in. And then afterward by sheer dint of his force of character, and his love of creation—if he's a creative individual—it all comes out his way.

But now don't get wrong this idea of individuality. You can see individuality in all these things, can't you? There's but one principle back of the thing we call a flower; there is only one principle back of this whole series, whole world of cacti. Only one principle; and it's the principle that you should study. You see these great elemental, basic things in nature that give the architect his certainty and his strength. Now he, of course, is like one of these things. He'll become a species, he'll become a feature of the flora, fauna, maybe, or whatever it is. That's open to him, as an architect, as a designer, as a maker of form. And he will understand *his* way, the thing that *he* has seen.

(November 28, 1954)

Architectural Design

In nature there is a continuous, ceaseless becoming. There is the great in-between of which Lao-tze speaks, which is alive, which never ceases to be. And into that realm of being you yourselves now stand or sit, hoping for something to arise within yourself which will respond to that great sea of becoming. Know that it is all rhythmical according to innate principles. And if you can tune in on those principles your hand will have direction and your mind will succeed in tracing something from within yourself that is there and alive and ready to become something when you call upon it properly. It is a moment which you could compare only with some deep religious devotion to a great ideal.

When you become the pencil in the hand of the infinite, when you are truly creative in your attempt to design, this thing that we call good design begins and never has an end. Once you are aware of the importance of this spirit living in nature, you will never have to copy nature. If you want to do a tree, you'll do your tree. You don't have to do a pine or an elm, you may do a tree of your own. You could make a squash that might end all squashes. And you might do all these things on a scale and to an extent that would be bigger than the nature that you see around you. You don't have to be the slave of that nature, because living in you is a higher form of feeling than can exist in the vegetable kingdom, the animal kingdom, or any other kingdom. By way of it your own individuality will find its own fruition.

Now we use that word "fruition" in the sense of true realization. What is reality? Reality, of course, consists in self-realization. The animals have it in some form or other, on a lower level. The birds have it, the fishes have it, everything in nature has it. The trees, the flowers, the vegetables here piled up in front of us all have it. We have it as a gift in a higher sense, as a spiritual quality which can make of life something more beautiful, more harmonious, lift it above anything else in nature. So to descend to an imitative level in this process of design would be stupid. But that stupidity is what we witness almost always.

There is another aspect of the word "organic" that's important to architectural design. We do not define organic principles inherent in nature by way of taste. Taste is only a matter of ignorance, which is difficult to make people understand. The word "taste" is exactly what it means— you taste and you like or you taste and you spit out. It's the same in the realm of the ordinary designer. By way of his taste he goes here or he goes there or he does this or he does that. The word "organic" to him would be an anathema. The idea that there are eternal principles that must be known in order to bear good fruit would be obnoxious to him. And he would resent the term organic in relation to artistic expression. For him organics is a harness, a bridle, a regulation of the spirit by way of knowledge. Knowledge is always both a liberation and a constraint. It's like conscience. Freedom without conscience would result usually in jail—the ordinary designer should be incarcerated before very long.

What must you do in the realm of design? When you sit down before this blank sheet of paper, you must have some knowledge and you must be guided by that knowledge toward an end as fanciful and imaginative as you see it to be in nature. Nature never has to repeat a form. She hates to. She takes great pains to preserve a species, but she'll never cease endeavoring to differentiate that species: see the human race, see all the animals, see the shells, the fishes, the trees and the flowers. Although nature will manage to preserve the species at all costs, she will differentiate, as when she implanted the sex principle in human beings. And why did she make man and woman? Why did she not leave one original? She did it to get variety, to evolute the species, to transcend the one pattern; to have richness of life which consists always in differentiation, in individuality.

I am what they call an individualist because I believe it to be inherent in the organic character of this universe as design. We ourselves are a part of it, participate in it. That participation in the depths of nature is really the function and privilege of the artist. What will make you an artist is the capacity to get deep into that sense of nature. So, first of all an artist is a student of nature, in that sense. He becomes so by way of his growth during his years of endeavor. And it takes years, it's not a flashy thing. He becomes more or less a component part of that mind in nature of which his own mind is but a reflection. His own mind is only to the great mind of nature what theat pine needle is to the principle of the tree. And when that sense of the greatness of his function comes to him, he becomes worthy of the name of artist.

Of course that has been so far gone nowadays by way of taste and willful performance and shallow pretense and all of the things that disintegrate instead of solidifying, that we have what we have today. And I can't see anything that is worthy of very great respect in architecture. We seem to have come along this line of civilization more and more bereft of the godhead which would eventuate into what might be called good design.

Now why? Abuse, of course. You can't abuse anything long and get away with it. If you comprehend and strive to live up to your comprehension, eventually you will grow. But if you indulge and are satisfied you will not. . . .

You all want to design things. You want to learn how to design things. Well, you don't learn how to design things by sitting at a drafting board with a pencil in your hand, and with T-square and triangle. That's what this talk this morning chiefly means, and that's why I'm giving it to you. I never sit down to a drawing board—and this has been a life-long practise of mine—until I have the whole thing in my mind. I may alter it substantially, I may throw it away, I may find I'm up a blind alley; but unless I have the idea of the thing pretty well in shape, you won't see me at a drawing board with it.

But all the time I have it it's germinating, between three o'clock and four o'clock in the morning—somehow nature has provided me with an hour or more of what might be called insight. Anyway the whole thing comes in revision, and I have it in my mind, and it will turn over and over, and then I'll go to sleep for a couple of hours. And in the morning what troubled me and I didn't have, I have.

So this design matter is not something to do with a drawing board. It is something that you do as you work, as you play. You may get it in the middle of the tennis court and drop your racket and run off and put it down. That is the kind of thing that it is. It is fleeting, it is evanescent. It's up here where you have to be quick and take it.

(September 12, 1953)

Tenuity

"Tenuity" was a term Frank Lloyd Wright used frequently to describe his work. For him tenuity meant that by steel reinforcing embedded in concrete, one could "push and pull" on a building. That was the principle that saved the Imperial Hotel during the devastating earthquake that leveled all the rest of Tokyo and Yokohama in 1923, and from that time on it became the dominant structural principle in his work. Out of it came, naturally, the cantilever—the projecting roof or floor slab supported in from the edges. And out of the cantilever came the elimination of the walled perimeter and its constricting corners. This box-destruction then gave rise to a sense of interior space flowing from within outward, a sense of the exterior and the interior merging as one.

You've heard me talk about tenuity 'til I'm black in the face. What is tenuity? That's the new thing in building. No ancient architect and no ancient builder ever had it. He could only make superimpositions of materials upon materials. When you could make several materials become as one, and weld them together from within, you got what we call the principle of tenuity, which built the Imperial Hotel. It brought it through the earthquake and it now can take the guttersnipe concrete blocks, out of the gutter and weld them all together so that you can pull on the building so. That never happened in the architecture of the world until we got steel.

Well now the little do-it-yourself house we call the Usonian Automatic is taking advantage of the principle of tenuity steel rods in the joints, laid so that the building is homogenous vertically and horizontally and virtually indestructible. And when that grooved edge on the block came into play you could dispense with skilled labor, because all you have to do now is to lay tier of blocks on tier of blocks. And in the joints vertically the rods are standing up. The blocks go between, and you slip in the horizontal rod, and then a boy comes with teapot full of grout and pours that horizontal joint. And it does run in because we've broken down sections of wall to see now completely that horizontal joint would be filled; and it's seldom failed to be filled. So here you have automatically a dispensation in building which eliminates skilled labor. A house can now be built by way of the patterns that you make and the diagrams that you furnish to the superintendent of the building—this case it will be the owner himself probably, a G.I. say. He can build this thing himself.

Apprentice: Mr. Wright, is that principle of tenuity a new idea of yours, or has that been used before in architecture?

My dear boy, it's no idea of mine. It's a perception of mine, that's all. I perceived it and put it to work in the concrete block.

Apprentice: Does it hold in the old architecture too, the Gothic . . .

No, of course not. The old architecture didn't have steel. The old architecture is one thing on another thing, the piling up of building materials with no coherent relationship to each other. You could not pull on those buildings. The moment the earthquake would come, or any disturbing force, they would fall apart. But with this element of tenuity imbedded, it cannot fall apart. It's an entirely new principle, motivated by the simple fact that a steel rod now is the most economical means of resisting the decay and the destruction of a building that could be imagined. When you can pull on the building, floors and walls, and when it has become homogenous, become one, that's a great fact in the history of architecture.

Now that great fact began to be made manifest when I got hold of this idea that a building could now be plastic. Plasticity came into building with tenuity, see. The forms of the old building were all based upon what? It was the box, of course. And the rigidity and strength of the building consisted in the strength and resistance of the corners of the building, which were the life of the building. Well, with the principle of tenuity and play the corner no longer means anything to the building except wide spans. If you're going to span from corner to corner, or build from corner to corner, you are certainly compelled to make longer spans than you would if you could bring the support that was the corner in from the corner. That way you create a cantileverage so that the overhang you create out here helps hold up the load. Should have a diagram here now, but do you get what I mean?

Let's see, here's the old wall and here's your corner support. Your spans are all from corner to corner. Now suppose that this corner which was here was moved into there, the support. Now whatever this projects reduces the span on this side and you get a support under the center of a load. Instead of grabbing the end of a load this way, you're under it and supporting it. Well now when you take that principle of support, creating a cantileverage here overhead, all this corner can be thrown out. Here's where your support is in on each side *from* the corner, and the corner becomes an open space.

You understand it? Simple as one, two, three, A, B, C. Right in that simple act, the whole formation of a building changes. You see now how when you move the support from the corner, in along on the wall, and you have steel—you couldn't do this thing without steel—you throw the whole thing into tension. The construction of your building now has tenuity as its principle instead of superimposition—one thing on another.

(June 27, 1954)

The Unit System

Apprentice: Mr. Wright, will you tell us about the unit system.

Do you see that rug on the floor in front of you? That was of course fabricated on the unit system. No unit system, no rug. The warp is spaced according to design, and then on the warp come the stitches taken according to design, and it is merely a yardstick to insure good scale so that you will always have the whole thing in one consistent picture. That is its use in architecture, when you work on a unit system. In a sense a building is more difficult to build that way, because you have to be perfectly accurate when you use the unit system. The original layout has to be punctilious and perfect or else there is always trouble. But once done, the benefit to be derived from the unit system is it's the best way to build a building economically. Not only is it economical but it insures good proportions. Because when you have the unit system established, every part of the building is sure to be in perfect accord with every other part.

The unit system has that advantage to start with. There are many other advantages. As you can see the consistent harmony in the pattern of the rug, so you see in a building constructed on the unit system a certain harmonious pattern. Too, it gives a certain integrity to the whole thing; you get the effect of it although you don't see what's happened.

I began using the unit system in small houses in Oak Park in the early days. I don't know what started me on it, but I found that after I had been using it for a good many years that the Beaux Arts always practised it and that it was a Beaux Arts system. All these magnificent plans of theirs, all these grand, elegant schemes were all worked out on the unit system. So I dare say that the unit system went way back to, perhaps, the days of the Renaissance, although I have never seen any plans.

The important thing in the unit system is adopting a unit which is appropriate to what you want to do. How you arrive at the unit system you want to use has been predetermined for you, in a way, by the building material suppliers, the people who make something for you 4 by 8. The 4 by 8 in timber sizes determines practically your spacing. So it's always wise in making your plan to take the unit which is most appropriate to the materials which you have to use. In the early days I was not bound too much by those things because of using concrete. We didn't depend so much on timber and these plastic sheets that are now made, like plywood and the like. If you are going to use these standardized materials you have got to use the standardized unit or else you are going to get into very extravagant measures before you get through. But I don't see any reason why you cannot subdivide them or multiply them. You can split the thing down the middle; there are many ways.

The main thing in determining the unit system, which should come out of your own experience, is the scale of the building in relation to the human figure, and the relation to the uses to which it will be put. Now that means your door openings, it means your windows, there are so many things that enter into the adoption of the proper unit that you have to give that a very careful consideration before you put it on a drawing board. What shall the spacing be? And, of course, you are always tied back into the standard stock of materials by which you want to build a building. To be free of those is very desirable, but as the things are going now here are your concrete blocks, all made according to a certain unit system, and that system is the 4 by 8 system, which is also 2 by 4. So that practically you are down in building now to the 2 by 4 or the 4 by 8, and so it goes.

The unit system was used in horizontal plan by the Beaux Arts, but they never used it vertically. They never used a vertical unit system, which I used in Oak Park and which I have used in all these houses. You can vary that according to the human scale or you vary it according to your materials. When I used the unit system in the concrete block system—I called it the textile block system—it was sixteen inches. I was trying to get a man-handled unit which about right for one man to pick up and put on a wall. That unit system can always be varied according to your materials or the effect you want to get. But you should also have the unit system vertical because it's valuable and probably even more necessary if you want to compose your building in good proportion. The unit system then is as basic architecture as the warp is to this rug. And for the same reason. A pattern of the whole depends upon the unit system, and the felicity is yes, facility. The whole building operation depends on how appropriate your unit system is to that circumstance.

Apprentice: Mr. Wright, what would determine the shape of the unit?

You can have it square, you can have it diagonal, you can go through all the figures of geometry if you want to. The first change from the square unit system, probably in history, was the Hanna house, which I designed on the basis of the honeycomb. That is the first time the honeycomb ever came into the unit system where building was concerned. I tried that experiment because I thought that after all the square with its angles was not particularly human, not very well adapted to circulation, to moving about in the building. That worked out very well.

Well, if you can use it as a honeycomb, you can use it as a diamond, you can use it as a triangle, you can use it as a circle. The hexagon is a very fruitful unit to use. The Unitarian Church is all done on a triangle, and many of our buildings today, I would say most of them, can be resolved either into a triangle or into a diamond. But there is no limit to the pattern as I see it now.

(July 30, 1952)

Constructing the One Room House

Suppose you wanted to design a one room house, which is a problem I'm going to give you now, to turn out a one room house. We've got to turn out a one room house that can be built for $5,000 and have in it nearly everything that they have now for $12,500 or over. You can't, of course, put a big family in a one room house. Yet I believe you could encompass almost everything that would make a big family happy, except quiet. I think you could arrange for decency, but not quiet.

That's been the kind of house I've been approaching all these years, throwing out room after room after room, emphasizing and developing, even enlarging where that was needed. Now we've got to the point where the last act is to be performed. So we'll have one room. Of course one room is what a house amounts to anyway, isn't it, almost, except for little sleeping compartments. Families all live in a heap anyhow. You make rooms for the children, but they'll all be under mother's feet. They'll all tangle. Now the family tangle can be accommodated quite easily in one room. The question is, how to make that family tangle tolerable and decent.

It's something very well worth doing for an architect. I don't think it has been done. I've been turning it over and over and over until I feel that I can, by way of low partitions, accomplish the necessary, and at the same time keep the whole thing free. The little Adelman house gives you a hint when you see that kitchen related to the living room, when you see all that going up into the air. I see no reason why you can't accomplish the whole family need in some such fashion as that.

We'll say the house is 36 by 36. How many square feet is that— quick now. Thirteen hundred isn't it. Thirty-six by thirty-six, I think, can accommodate any G.I. family with not more than two children. When the third child comes, that begins to complicate things. But for the man and his wife and two children, 36 by 36 ought to do the trick. If it doesn't, you can add a few feet more. The design can be so made, of course, that you can add a wing to the thing, by extending the wing to one side where the bedroom naturally was. You have to have the plumbing, and the plumbing in a little thing like this could be combined with the bathroom, kitchen sink, and heating apparatus. The plumbing could almost be a prefabricated unit, designed so you could insert it in the thing, almost independent of the structure. And I think the ceiling could be independent of the partitions and be a free, open space, and very charming.

I think your little one story house could have more sense of spaciousness and charm of effect than almost any of the expensive houses.

Because those places you are tied down by one room the living room, and we've expanded it by throwing in the workspace.

(December 12, 1954)

House and Client

I think that the people who live in a house must understand the character and the nature of that house which was designed for them to live in. It's their duty to understand, to appreciate, and conform insofar as possible to the idea of the house. And that idea should be within their grasp. I've been guilty many times, and I have to confess it, of going way beyond the people who lived in the house. It's taken some many, many years to catch up. There are instances where the people who got the house in the first place messed it up gosh-awful. As they bought, and had money to buy things to put in the house, they bought the wrong things and put them in the wrong places.

Well, now, of course, it was their privilege—but was it? It certainly was not their best act. Everyone who has a house to live in is subject to the general character of that building. We're speaking of organic architecture now, not people who live in some preconceived style. There you have the argument for a style as against the individual thing. The individual thing is at once easier and more difficult than the other thing. Certainly safer is the cliche house which has been accepted and which has definite ways of doing everything to which people can be educated in herds and droves.

It's quite easy to bring that accusation—of going way beyond the grasp—against the architect who believes in the individual. He endeavors to give him a chance to develop that individuality in ways peculiar to himself. That's always the answer to this accusation which is eternal, will never cease. If the client is familiar with the organic processes of building a house, and if he has character, if he has choice, if he is an individual and expresses it definitely, it'll get into his house by way of his architect. But with it all comes something higher and better than he could ever have dreamed of doing himself. And he knows that it'll be there, and that's what he wants.

(September 7, 1958)

Creating Architecture: a State Capitol for Arizona

Have you seen the glad tidings, the news that the legislature of Arizona has approved the plans of the new State Capitol for Arizona? You may have seen it in the newspapers. It is a curious hybrid. It looks as though some young girls Culture Club had indulged in research and had come up with that design. It bears no resemblance whatever to a good honest expression of Arizona. It's a terrible, terrible thing.

Mr. Price suggested last night that the newspaper send an illustration to me of the capitol for my comment. And I said, "Why comment? The design is itself sufficient comment on Arizona without anything from me." But he said I should make a sketch now of what I think Arizona should have and send it to the newspaper as my comment. Good idea. But how many designs is a fellow good for?

Now what would be a representative expression of Arizona in the way of a building? It wouldn't be a New York skyscraper, would it? This is a New York skyscraper *[indicating newspaper]* buttressed by two other buildings one on each side. And then they put a dome on top of the skyscraper. What would occur to you, what would be the guiding principle, what would the thing essentially be if it was proper for Arizona as an emblem of Arizona's character. But in the location where it is now in the Valley of the Sun. That's where the capitol is going to stand, in the Valley of the Sun. So, of course, it would have to be something rather sheltered, umbrageous, and not this one, which is outrageous. I think that would be a slogan—umbrageous rather than outrageous.

Now of course your cranium is a dome, isn't it. Everyone of us is carrying a dome around, more or less good for something. But now for Arizona what would be an architectural motif suitable for the region and defined by just the simple word "appropriate"? What would be an appropriate capitol for the state of Arizona in the Valley of the Sun? There is a problem for you. What would you come up with?

What would you seek? What would you look for? Well, everybody has one answer in him, and those are good things to think about because that's what you're for. That will be your office in life as architects now, to find out, whenever a problem is presented to you: what is natural, significant, appropriate in the circumstances. Now of course nothing could be more inappropriate in the circumstances than what they have. Not possibly. If you were to sit down and try to think what would be the most damnable thing that Arizona could do to itself, what they have done would be it. Well, having succeeded in that direction, what would be in the other direction? Suppose they had come to you. Suppose any one of you wanted to sit down now and design a capitol for Arizona. What do you think you would do?

Apprentice: Mr. Wright, don't you think that the thing that would be characteristic of Arizona architecture is mainly that it is an outdoor architecture? It has lots of outdoor garden area and not very much hall space.

That's good. That's one condition, surely. Now what else?

Apprentice: Well, wouldn't it have a translucent roof over it. Mightn't it even be tentlike structure, have a translucent roof?

That's another idea that's good. Those two things put together make sense, don't they. What else?

Apprentice: Mr. Wright, I had the idea that the thing could be say, in the Papago Park area in those rocks. A series of huge terraces with tents on them that could be moved in the summertime to Flagstaff so that the government is not only temporary, it expresses the temporary condition of their office. It would move from one place to another.

I don't think that would ever go over. Have you ever counted the cost of moving something?

Apprentice: Well, if it was just a tent that had to be moved, it could be moved fairly easily.

Well, it is a circus in itself, but I doubt if you would ever succeed in getting it to recognize itself as a circus. And the movable tent is indissolubly associated in the public mind with a circus. These statesmen, you can tell by their wanting to put a dome on top of the skyscraper what they think of themselves. They've given themselves away very foolishly.

Now this is what we have to begin with. It is an arable area and is entitled to great spread in a climate that is not severe but is intense and will burn up anything in the summer. You can fry eggs out on the concrete there in July. Literally, crack them and fry them on the concrete. It's 118 in the summer and it's hot as hell. So something has to be done in the way of an overhead, doesn't it, that would enable you to use all this area for growth, plants, water. Water is a wonderful symbol of prosperity in Arizona, isn't it. Fountains, water, pools, everything, at least there would be one place where you could go and get a drink any time. It would be a great refreshing circumstance: water gardens, yes.

Now how about shelter? What kind of shelter? Is the dome a good form of shelter for Arizona? A great widespreading dome might be, provided that was made perforated, provided that was erected as a great overhead shelter for all that went on beneath it. And the buildings would be put beneath that shelter. First of all the overhead perforated shelter, casting beautiful shadows down below. Then put the Republicans over here and the Democrats there and give them their little pow-wow place, Senate, Assembly, and the public, of course, in the center. Then have wide-spread wings which would contain the offices of the legislators, again the Republicans on one side and the Democrats on the other side. You see, the whole nature of the design is a bifurcation—of what—not authority. Authority is central, but arriving at authority is dual, you see. Plus and minus or minus and plus, and it is naturally in two, the whole situation. The capitol dome in Washington has the House of Representatives on one side and the Senate on the other side, and in between they have all these halls for the public to come and view the legislators who have passed away and see clearly and definitely that their clothes did not fit them. That's at least a privilege the government offers in the great rotunda which they have. So it seems there should be a rotunda, a place where the public can come and inform itself as to the greatness of past statesmen compared with the insignificance of those they have now.

Then you go into the Senate. It seems a little strange that the Senate is on a footing with the Assembly, that the two balance each other, which, of course, they don't. The Senate has been strained from the Assembly, really, hasn't it. The senators are usually taken from the ranks of the congressmen, and it is the higher house, it is the senior house. I never thought there was anything quite just in an establishment that would recognize the Senate and the Assembly as one. But I don't think that you would ever get anywhere with a design that didn't put them on a parity. So that would be a feature in your design. You would have the two houses. You would have the *pro bono publico* Arizona to start with.

Then you would have the necessities of the congressmen meeting people in their offices, and you would have to be accessible from the two central chambers. They refer to them as chambers, and chambers they would have to be—with all kinds of easy access to committee meetings because all of these houses proceed by way of conferences. They appoint committees, committees for this, committees for that, committees for the other. So from the central chamber there would have to be access to all of these committee rooms. But in general effect, anything in the Valley of the Sun here would have to have a design totally different from anything in the north, in Minneapolis, for instance, and in Wisconsin, or anywhere else north of the Mason-Dixon line.

Well now, let's go on with it. What would be the shape of the thing? A great dome, a great shelter rising over everything, say four or five-hundred feet in diameter. With the chambers underneath it, themselves domed underneath a dome. How would that do? And the gardens flourishing, because if you want planting to grow and flourish in Arizona, if you put a lathe house over it, cover it up with some kind of protection, you get ten to one times beauty in your growth as if you left them bare in the sun. So all this sense of gardens and fountains and water could flourish under a great perforated canopy—won't call it a dome. And under the canopy you could put the domes of the legislators. And under the domes of the legislature, you could arrange all these things that they are peculiarly committed to do for the vox populi.

And it could be very big, very wide—ground is cheap in Arizona. You could make it occupy as many acres of ground as were available. And it would be a great circumstance and not so very expensive, either. You wouldn't waste very much on details, wouldn't have to. It would be more or less a great permanent tent of a circular character—or would you rather see it of a triangular character? Yes, you could work it out— the three points of the triangle. Here would be the legislature, here would be the congress, and here would be the *pro bono publico,* you see. You could do it in a triangle, in a circle. It could be either triangular or circular, I guess. And we've seen the circular form so much now that we can't really get rid of it. If you were to present a triangular form to those congressmen, they would immediately rebel. If you presented them with a great domicular form, they would immediately respond for the reason the dome has got fixed in the mind of *pro bono publico* as somehow indissolubly associated with authority.

(February 10, 1957)

Toward a New Architecture

Architecture has never had the opportunity it now has. Architecture today can be the great and revealing process of life and thought of the American people—and it's going to be, in fact I think it is. I think we are going to have architecture, I think we have got it on the way. If you'll compare what's happening now and what people demand to live with and live in—even government housing which is the worst in the world, probably. But I doubt if it's any worse than it used to be, and perhaps it has some features better than those that used to characterize the life.

In our humble period, when man was nothing, he was not an individual. He had virtually signed off either to a monarchy or signed off to a religious oliarchy. He was not free. Now if freedom means anything, it means an architecture of our own. It means what we are doing and it means that it is, eventually, universal. Yes sir, that much I'm sure of. The sixty-five years I've put in working at it comes out, at the end, with that faith. And I think it's a miracle so far as we've got. I may do a lot of griping and ridiculing—and I'm not very kind oftentimes, probably—but nevertheless my faith in the thing is just as great or greater than it ever was.

And I see results and so must everything. You see perversions too. It's hard to see the thing that grew, purely and straight from the shoulder at first, twisted off and glanced to the right and to the left. But it doesn't matter—that's all part of it. And eventually we're going to have the greatest architecture and the greatest sense of art in life that ever existed in the world.

We're headed in for it now. This place couldn't exist but for that fact. The work that I've done couldn't be done but for that fact. They say a prophet is without honor, save in his own country. Well, I doubt that; otherwise how have I built some 769 buildings with my own hands? What other country could that happen in? None in the world.

Don't you see, there's no occasion to do anything but to attend to our knitting and know where the values lie, know what's up and what's down, what's in and what's out, and work away. And the thing is coming in spite of any man, and because of man—because he is what he is. Because something has been given to him in this sense of romance, love of beauty. He's never going to let go of it. He's going to refine it and enlarge it, intensify it and continue to do that until what he builds is miraculous.

And we have the means. We're the only civilization, well let's say modern civilization, not American civilization but modern civilization having been given the great tool, the machine, to work with. And having been given these scientific accomplishments and revelations which should be used by us, we can go places no civilization ever went before or ever could go. Not that where we're going and what we're going to accomplish reflects upon them. It only proves something that was already there with them. And because it was there, now, with the new advantages and the fresh start we go way beyond where they stood, in one sense.

In another sense we never will, because when a man has blessed his age, his time and his human family by a sincere contribution to that life and its purposes, nothing ever goes beyond it. It may go beyond it in expediency at the time, it may go beyond it in availability, it may be ten to one what we would call practical. But the nature of the gift and the character of the giving is never lessened by anything that ever comes afterward. The measure of its nobility and its continuity is its depth of feeling and its sincerity. And if it has that quality, it stands.

(July 14, 1957)

The Nature of Materials: wood: Hillside Drafting Room, Taliesin, Spring Green, WI, 1935, detail of wood trusses

The Nature of Materials: stone: "Fallingwater," Edgar J. Kaufmann house, Mill Run, PA, 1935

The Nature of Materials: brick: Loren Pope house, Mount Vernon, VA, 1939

The Nature of Materials: glass: Frank Lloyd Wright study-bedroom, Taliesin, Spring Green, WI, 1925

The Nature of Materials: concrete: Solomon R. Guggenheim Museum, New York, NY, 1943

Project: Huntington Hartford Play Resort, Hollywood, CA, 1947

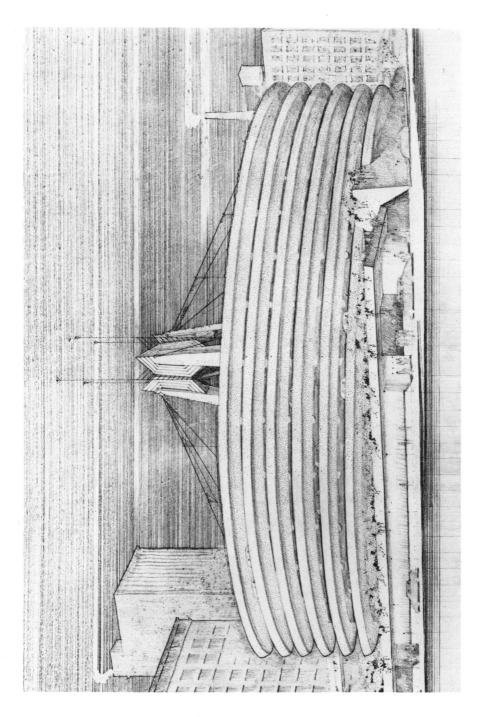

Project: Self-Service Garage for Edgar J. Kaufmann, Pittsburgh, PA, 1949

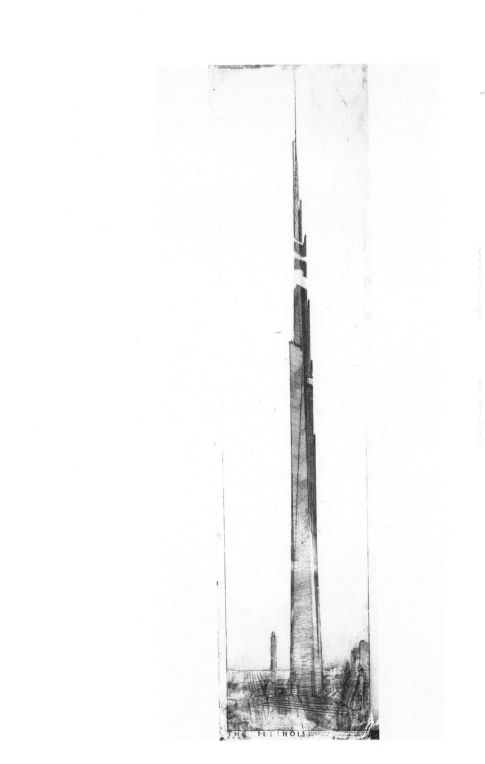

Project: Mile High Illinois, Chicago, IL, 1956

PART FIVE

A SUMMING UP

Sometimes the Sunday talks were so tightly integrated and at the same time so various in theme and context as to defy excerpting or classification. Instead they reflected the whole man—his life, thoughts, world, and universe—in rich abundance. "Really To Believe in Something" is such a talk, and it is presented on the following pages. "The Master Poet" is another such talk and, as pointed out in the Preface, it occupies Side Four of the cassette tapes. It is omitted from the text, however, leaving you, the reader, alone with the living voice of Frank Lloyd Wright. That way we hope to recreate, at least in part, the first hand experience of those Sunday talks.

Really To Believe in Something

I think you are so lucky not facing the light—that's a very bad proposition architecturally. I hope it will all sink into you. Never design houses where people have to sit facing the light. If you're sideways you can turn your head and see. And that's the best way. That's the way it should be. Unfortunately every building has four sides. That's the beauty of the triangle. With the triangle you can manage it so that nobody has to sit facing the light. Lay it out on paper some time, and you'll see.

Well, what do all of you want to talk about this morning? There are a lot of you here now. I'm getting rather frightened. I'm not accustomed to being in such a large company. Pretty hard to cover you all. But you're all here with practically the same intent, from very different angles, no doubt, and very different sources of inspiration. Because all of you are inspired, aren't you? Inspired by what, when, or how, that's the question. But inspired you all are with some desire, some intent, some deep felt wish—which is a prayer, you know. A prayer is nothing but a deep felt wish. I think a prayer should always be silent, and probably mostly is. What you're praying for most, you know best.

And yet I've been surprised frequently by boys who really had a deep felt wish and were unaware of it. They were mostly the ones who had been educated. They'd been taught a prayer or the equivalent of one which they would recite while feeling entirely something else. Well, I hope that isn't true of any of you, because I can't think of a fix more detrimental to the ambition of the young architect than to straddle the fence like that. To have deep in his heart one wish and to have to conform to the conditions and demands of another. That's what makes a bad marriage and will also make a bad architect. You have to go wholeheartedly into anything in order to achieve anything worth having. And if your allegiance is divided, if your thought is divided, if your feeling is confused, get rid of that condition as soon as you can and light on something else.

Really to believe in something is the greatest boon, I think, and to believe wholeheartedly in it and to serve it with all your strength and your might is salvation, really. And in this day it's so hard to come by and so few people ever arrive at it that it's almost negligible—certainly in educational circles. Because in the higher education circles they are presented with so many confusing thoughts and ideas that there is no clear one for them to think when they finish their course. They are full of dregs like a wine that isn't fit to drink.

Well, that's a preliminary now, and you can enlarge upon it. How about it? Anybody with a personal experience, any one who has been through the mill, discovered the things we've been talking about, discovered them to be true. I never liked that saying of Pilate's, What is truth? The answer to that is simple very simple: what is natural. Now then comes the question again, what is natural? What is nature, natural? It would be organic, of course, wouldn't it? And organic, again, would be a good word to use in connection with that ideal you are seeking. And that is why we have it here, why we call it "organic" architecture.

Let's take up that word this morning and thrash it out. What is organic? What would be organic? Something hanging in the butcher shop is organic, a dead carcass of a pig or a live one there, for that matter, is organic. But there is another phase, another sense to this term organic. That one is what is profoundly interrelated, one thing to another, consistent as a whole. That's organic in the sense we use it. So when I say that architecture is organic, I mean the whole is to the part as the part is to the whole. It is consistently one thing, especially for the purpose for which it was designed. That ties you down pretty flat and it's pretty hard to get away from it. And when it really possesses you and really gets hold of you, you're on the road to doing something good. Now it may not seem good to your neighbors, it may not seem good to the man next to you, but if it's good to you in the organic sense, it will prove to be good in the course of time.

My own experience is bearing that out for your benefit. I started with this *[organic architecture]* some sixty-five years ago, and it's growing better and better and stronger and stronger all over the world. Why? Because it is according to the laws and principles of what is natural. Artificiality can only be carried so far, and is carried so far by most of us that it seems the natural thing. There is our difficulty in culture, in education—being able to distinguish, to discriminate, between what is our natural state and what it is that has been foisted upon us by education, which is artificiality all down the line.

To be natural doesn't mean to be a savage. To be natural doesn't mean to be crude. To be natural simply means to know which is the right side up and which is wrong side up. And to have it in your hearts as an inheritance from, well, let's say, on high, justifies your thought to you. And there you are with the possession of something precious to defend which, let's say, is your own conviction. You can be wrong of course. Many of the most "convictous" persons in the world have been deadly wrong. There was Hitler for instance, and a great many examples whom you could name, people who felt that they were right but who were absolutely wrong.

In all of us there is a quality, a little something, I think it's referred to as a still small voice. I've heard it all my life. Listen to the still small voice of conscience. A man's conscience is really the mainspring of what he, with some reason, might call his soul. So listen attentively to conscience, always. Freedom without it is dangerous and will land you in jail. Your conscience is your guiding star and the finest thing about you in principle, where manhood or womanhood is concerned. Now, putting it in terms of organic architecture, the good building of good design is what squares up with what I've just defined as a good conscience. It's where the materials you use are understood and lovingly and correctly used as materials. Where the design you make has in it the properties of truth, and that means a design that is appropriate and square for the purpose for which it was intended. You know exactly why the shape of a thing is that shape, and you know how far to go with it and how far not to go. But that's something that will take you a long term of years to be really sure of. That's the most difficult thing to face as young architects.

That we can sum up in what you might call a sense of proportion. A sense of proportion is a conscientious realization of limitation. That's a good definition, and you won't find it in a dictionary. For the designer good conscience is the fruit of much serious devotion, study, and experience. All you can expect of youngsters, of young fellows, in that connection is a desire, a feeling that they want the best, the highest, and the truest, and are willing to make sacrifices to get it. That's where it's first manifest. Then it grows and grows and grows, until after a while the very thing you do and the very thing you see becomes more and more the thing that you are. It becomes a conscientious liberation in terms of human feeling, of how you live, what you live in, what you live for. In other words: architecture.

I think that the architecture that the world is seeing today is mostly architecture by instinct, architecture by an innate sense of the thing we are talking about. But nowhere in the world, I believe, has it been specifically laid out in terms of accomplishment. It's had all sorts of names, you know. There was the Gothic, which we would say came close, not too close; Byzantine, closer; and of the Oriental Gothics, Persian probably the closest of all. Then comes the Orient proper: Chinese architecture, native, characteristic, brother of the pine; the pine tree is the original of the Chinese temple.

Out of environment, out of all that surrounds the human being, he derives a certain strength of imagery, of imagination. It belongs more to nature than to education. And he can't get at the sound that comes from the drum by cutting out the head of it, which is what education has been trying to do all these years. What he can do is study the nature of his environment. He can study the nature of whatever attracts his attention. And as I have so often said, he can soon get the practise of looking into the thing instead of just at it. And looking in he'll always see these relationships I've been talking about that will appeal to his artist-conscience. His artistic conscience will gradually develop and save him from being foolish and save him from betraying his clients and save him from adding to the errors which now disgrace this country, and I would say the whole world as regards what is being done in the name of architecture.

All of this is religious. Yes, all of this is square with true religion, but not with sectarianism. And all of this is square with science. But science is the lower form, the lower stratum, the physical means only by which to approach these ideals and concepts which are creative. Science does not offer very great contact with the things of the spirit or with depths of being, which really is the same thing. We are too quickly enamored by, and have been overloaded and pushed to the brink of destruction by, our devotion to science and our inability to understand what we've left out by way of art, architecture, and religion. There is no architecture that isn't religious. There is no artistic feeling independent of religion.

Religion has many definitions and comes in many packages, as many almost as the stuff you see in the market. And it is that confusion of thought and confusion in our lives that renders nearly everything we do commonplace, ineffective—perhaps a little of this or a little of that, but nothing really fine, noble, and convincing as a whole. To get the near end of this thing into your systems, you've got to have a feeling toward architecture that is really religion. I'm sure that if there is a definition of religion that is really sound and true, it means just the things I've been talking about now. And to refer to it as a sectarian affair is of course to refer to our weakness. To talk of beauty as one thing, to talk of Unitarianism as another thing and all the rest of it, is all a blind floundering around, trying to get to the core of a truth so simple that they won't take it. It isn't good enough. It won't support all these divisions and various processions in the direction of something or other, somewhere, somehow, sometime.

So the architect must be master in the interior sense, not only of his tools, not only of his materials, but also of the human spirit. The soul of humanity is in his charge really. If that civilization to which he belongs is to really endure long upon the face of the earth he must eventually realize that architecture is to him his religion. Not only his religion, but the core of all religion. That of course seems high-falutin' and takes you far afield from where you want to go. Most of you will build something for your egoistic selves, but I believe that if you take this thing seriously enough and take it to heart and really get that feeling for it into your system, you'll emerge. It may take time, years perhaps, but eventually you'll produce something invaluable to your race and to your kind.

Don't let it bother you if they say you are making a religion out of architecture, because you are and you should. And the more you do it, the better will be the architecture. After all, boys, the main thing about it all is that you will be so much better. What it will do for you is something tremendous. To have a loyalty at heart for a cause that is deep and profound will make your sense of yourself as a man, will give your manhood a fine—I was going to say refuge because you'll need it oftentimes—but a fine stance. You'll be square on your spiritual feet and they can't push you around. And after a while you'll begin to know the right side up from the right side down and the wrong side up.

Well, that's a little sermon this morning and I apologize, but it was coming to you and now you've had it. So let's now go on and walk over the hills and see what's over the mountain there on the other side. How many of you are capable of getting over on the other side? I'm afraid I couldn't now unless I was hauled or ridden over, but over there is something beautiful. When I was a boy I read a book called *Arney, Arney Sol Bakken.* In that little book Arney was always wondering what was over there, over the mountains. Arney couldn't sleep for what was over the mountains until one day, in spite of everything and everybody, he packed up, put a knapsack on his back, and started out for over there. And Arney never came back. And nobody ever knew what he found.

(December 7, 1958)

We'll go up where we went before, and maybe a little farther . . .

Taliesin

Frank Hloyd Wright

March 22, 1959